T0114783

Praise For The Difference

"This remarkable anthology offers true inspiration for us to connect with hope in humanity and become wiser beings. The beautiful, life-changing and profound stories in this book are a must-read."

Dr. Edith Shiro, author of *The Unexpected Gift of Trauma: the path to Posttraumatic Growth.*

"Ten deeply personal stories about loss, courage and transformation that will inspire you and help you look at your own life differently. Each story is unique and yet all speak to the strength and resiliency of the human spirit."

Eva Ritvo, MD, psychiatrist, author, and co-founder of *The Bold Beauty Project.*

"This beautiful anthology of personal stories, edited by Rosemary Ravinal and Achim Nowak, captivates the reader with a profound sense of purpose, courage, and resilience. With each intimate, passionate account of life's journey, you're sure to unlock the authentic version of yourself. *The Difference* is a must-read for anyone seeking inspiration and fulfillment in life!"

Dana P. Rowe, musical theater composer, author, and leadership coach.

"These powerfully vulnerable stories in *The Difference* remind me that one of the most profound tools of the healing trades is the affirmation of our human capacity to transform pain into purpose. I am deeply touched by the authors' journeys and inspired by their transformations. Their stories are a gift of hope and possibility."

Dr. Linda Lausell Bryant, Associate Dean for Academic Affairs, NYU Silver School of Social Work.

"A true treasure! These stunning personal stories of strength, courage, and hope are exactly what we need today to inspire us to reach for the stars. They assure us that we can do it!"

Patricia Gussin, New York Times best-selling author of *Medicine and Mayhem: The Dr. Laura Nelson Files.*

"*The Difference* is life changing. It's no surprise that when I received the summary of the book to review I was going through a time of enormous stress and loss. Perfect timing. Just the advanced copy helped me to get grounded in truth and find some peace in one of the most difficult times in my life. Thank you for this book."

Jordan Adler, dream broker and author of the best-selling book, *Beach Money.*

"The honesty and raw beauty of the writing in *The Difference* touched me deeply. It compelled me to consider all the choices I have made in my own life. What a wise and inspiring book it is!"

Luis Gallardo, founder & president, World Happiness Foundation.

"We all fear loss and change, but ultimately life interruptions press us to move in new and more fulfilling directions. *The Difference* will inspire you to clarify your goals and dreams now."

Susan Ford Collins, bestselling author of *Blur: Clear the Way Ahead... even in the worst of times; The Joy Of Success and Our Children Are Watching.*

THE DIFFERENCE

Essays on Loss, Courage, and Personal Transformation

Achim Nowak & Rosemary Ravinal

BALBOA.PRESS

A DIVISION OF HAY HOUSE

Balboa Press books may be ordered through booksellers or by contacting:

Balboa Press
A Division of Hay House
1663 Liberty Drive
Bloomington, IN 47403
www.balboapress.com
844-682-1282

Because of the dynamic nature of the Internet, any web addresses or links contained in this book may have changed since publication and may no longer be valid. The views expressed in this work are solely those of the author and do not necessarily reflect the views of the publisher, and the publisher hereby disclaims any responsibility for them.

The author of this book does not dispense medical advice or prescribe the use of any technique as a form of treatment for physical, emotional, or medical problems without the advice of a physician, either directly or indirectly. The intent of the author is only to offer information of a general nature to help you in your quest for emotional and spiritual well-being. In the event you use any of the information in this book for yourself, which is your constitutional right, the author and the publisher assume no responsibility for your actions.

Any people depicted in stock imagery provided by Getty Images are models, and such images are being used for illustrative purposes only. Certain stock imagery © Getty Images.

New Living Translation (NLT)
Holy Bible, New Living Translation, copyright © 1996, 2004, 2015 by Tyndale House Foundation. Used by permission of Tyndale House Publishers, Inc., Carol Stream, Illinois 60188. All rights reserved.

Print information available on the last page.

ISBN: 979-8-7652-4142-4 (sc)
ISBN: 979-8-7652-4143-1 (e)

Library of Congress Control Number: 2023908125

Balboa Press rev. date: 05/04/2023

Contents

Foreword by Bruce Turkel vii

Introduction xi

Essays on Loss

Carl Ficks, Jr., Rage Against the Dying of the Light 1

Dr. Betsy Guerra, Finding Your Way Back to Joy 13

Rosemary Ravinal, The Return to a Homeland
That Wasn't.. 26

Reflections on Loss by **Rosemary Ravinal**...........................35

Essays on Courage

Alisa Sample-Alexander, Unveiling My Authentic Self....41

Dr. Lynne Maureen Hurdle, How Breaking Culture
Freed My Soul..52

Malissa Smith, How Boxing Uncaged Me............................ 62

Caroline de Posada, The Courage to Change Your
Choices 74

Reflections on Courage by **Achim Nowak** and
Rosemary Ravinal.. 86

Essays on Personal Transformation

Dr. Tom Garcia, Roar at the Moon 92

Mark J. Silverman, My Road to Healing 105

Achim Nowak, When I Was Willing To Try Anything........114

Reflections on Personal Transformation by **Achim Nowak**.. 129

Acknowledgements... 133
Biographies... 135
Contributors.. 137

Foreword

I was honored when Rosemary and Achim generously asked me to write a foreword to their book, *The Difference: Essays on Loss, Courage, and Personal Transformation*. First, because I have such warm regard for the two of them. But also because I think there's so much insightful value packed between their book's covers that we all need to consider and understand.

What moves me so profoundly about this anthology is that it's not only instructive and prescriptive, but also restorative. Rosemary and Achim have done us an enormous favor by tackling the yeoman's task of collecting universally relevant tales and presenting them to us in a thoughtful and organized manner. These are stories that we can all use as mirrors to our own experiences, guideposts for our future life travels, and soothing salves for our souls.

How do I know this? Even before I journeyed through all the stories, the headings for the book's three main sections—*Loss, Courage,* and *Personal Transformation*—prepared me for the voyage. The first heading is something that all of us have experienced and will continue to experience. The second two headings are attributes we all need to develop.

Oscar Wilde cautioned us, "To live is the rarest thing in the world. Most people exist, that is all." Thanks to our authors' insightful work, we can discover how to elevate our own lives beyond the uninspired norm decried by Wilde. Throughout this book, the stories have the power to inspire us to turn our losses into springboards to the better life for which we all yearn.

When I was a little boy, anytime my brother, sister, or I would complain about something we didn't have, my grandmother Mollie would say, "Don't compare." Having come to the United States as a small child with a family escaping the violent pogroms of Eastern Europe, Mollie believed that the only way to live her life was to look forward to and savor every small pleasure that came her way. According to my grandmother, each person's life was exclusively their own, complete with personal triumphs, failures, hopes, dreams, and disappointments. Mollie's empathetic worldview shaped my own.

Remembering my grandmother's admonishments helped me as I read *The Difference*. Instead of observing other people's stories from the comfortable distance between me and the page, I was able to experience their losses and discover new ways of dealing with my own memories of loss.

Like you, I have lost important people in my life, but not with the drama that Carl Ficks, Jr. experienced. Nor have I been uprooted from the country of my birth as Rosemary Ravinal was. Still, their stories of love and loss gave me new ways of looking at what I have lost and what has been taken from me as well as what I still hold dear.

Similarly, I have never stepped into a boxing ring like Malissa Smith. Nor have I had to overcome cultural parenting norms the way Dr. Lynne Maureen Hurdle did. Yet, reading their stories of bravery gave me new insights into what others have done to overcome their obstacles and challenges. My fondest hope is that their tales have begun to backfill a wellspring of courage that I can draw on when I need that quality the most.

Finally, the collected stories of transformation had additional significance for me because I have been thinking and writing about this subject for a while. My latest book, *Is That All There Is?*, explored how successful people change their lives for the better. All three people featured in the Personal Transformation section of the book you're about to read—Mark J. Silverman, Dr. Tom Garcia, and Achim Nowak—supplemented my recent research and added to my quiver of viable strategies and proven techniques for creating fundamental change in my own life.

Without a doubt, these conversations cover difficult issues. Facing these crossroads in your life might seem to be a daunting task, but don't worry. Both Rosemary and Achim have accepted the responsibility to serve as your casting directors and tour guides. Doing this, they've assembled a group of people who have lived through the sorts of experiences that best-selling authors and award-winning screenwriters spend a lifetime searching for. And then they've stitched their stories together into a compelling narrative that will help you navigate your own journey and find your way to the mountaintop.

In fact, one of Mark Silverman's practices might be your best directive for continuing through the pages that await you. When Silverman tells us to "consume uplifting and inspiring content," he could very well be talking about reading *The Difference*.

And as Dr. Tom Garcia shares in his story of redemption, you are never alone. Although Garcia is writing about the many forms of support he found throughout his own travails, he likewise could just as accurately have been referencing this volume.

Thanks to Achim and Rosemary's gentle guidance, you too can relive the darker parts of your life's journey, find meaning deep within them, and emerge triumphantly into the light. And even with my grandmother's words ("Don't compare!") ringing in my ears, I envy your upcoming journey of discovery.

– Bruce Turkel
Author, Corporate Branding Expert, and Hall of Fame Speaker

Introduction

This anthology began with a deceptively simple premise: what forces have made a difference in the lives of successful and influential people?

We are blessed to know many gifted and fascinating humans and began to assemble a group of possible contributors with vastly different life stories. We were honored with the enthusiastic response to our request for unvarnished personal memoirs about life-changing shifts, triggers and catalysts that made a difference in their life trajectories.

We selected eight storytellers. Each one has experienced loss, faced dramatic personal transformation, and demonstrated courage beyond measure. Individually and collectively, they inspire millions of followers around the world to lead more authentic, wholehearted, and expansive lives.

The questions we posed were meant to prompt honest reflection and offer real-life examples to inspire others.

- *If you were to pinpoint the ONE factor or experience that invoked the greatest personal transformation in your life, what comes to mind?*
- *What made the biggest difference and left a lasting effect?*
- *What sort of explorations do you suggest for others who may desire to make a conscious and profound change?*

The personal narratives we received from our eight contributors thrilled us and motivated us to add our own essays.

We invited colleagues who we knew to be both superb writers and exceptional thinkers, and this is, indeed, what they delivered. Their stories are presented here in their own words. Their writings capture their unique voices: highly personal, vulnerable, raw, and deep. Their insights into how their lives transformed resound with timeless and transcendent wisdom and offer lessons for anyone who seeks a rich, purposeful, and fulfilling life.

As we combed through these marvelous essays, it quickly became evident that there were three shared themes. The biggest surprise, perhaps, was how many of our authors wrote about loss in its many forms – the loss of a fellow human being, the loss of an identity, the loss of a culture, the loss of a long-held belief – and how our resolve to embrace and move through the pain and grief of loss irrevocably impacts everything that follows.

We kept returning to the experience of loss as THE singular galvanizing force for some of our authors. We received multiple stories about unexpected personal courage, and how the courage to follow "the road less traveled" yielded extraordinary returns. And we found stories that mirrored the archetypal hero's journey through darkness into a deep spiritual awakening. Here is what's in store for you in this anthology.

THEME 1: LOSS

Carl Ficks, Jr. had an impressive career of over three decades as an attorney, partner in multiple law firms, and head of corporate and donor relations for a hospital. A series of painful personal losses challenged Carl to face an uncomfortable truth: He was done with practicing law. In his essay "Rage Against the Dying of the Light," Carl describes how his encounter with multiple losses propelled him to pursue an entirely different line of work that mines his untapped passions.

For Dr. Betsy Guerra, a psychotherapist, counselor, and author, the tragic death of her young daughter in 2013 forever changed the course of her life. It moved Betsy to closely examine the powerful relationship she had to her religious faith. It also helped her realize that she had tools that had served her. As she entered the vibrant next phase of her life that embraced her grief, she used the same tools to counsel families facing their own losses.

Co-editor Rosemary Ravinal left Cuba at the age of seven in the first wave of exiles fleeing the regime of Fidel Castro. Though she made a prosperous life, raised a daughter, and had a thriving career as a communications professional and media personality in the United States, she is haunted by thoughts of her homeland and a cultural bereavement she cannot reconcile. Her desire for Cuban identity remains a nagging source of loss and longing.

THEME 2: COURAGE

Alisa Alexander is a woman of many gifts. She is a performer who can be heard on many gospel recordings, a keynote speaker, an exceptional classroom facilitator, and a professional instructional designer. In Alisa's life, these gifts were expressed in parallel lanes until one extraordinary day, when she was speaking in front of an audience of more than a thousand people and spirit moved her to sing. In an instant of courage, the separation into different paths and multiple facets of Alisa was banished.

Dr. Lynne Maureen Hurdle, a luminary in the conflict resolution world, credits the courageous act of "breaking culture" as a singular moment in her personal liberation. Raised in an African American culture with traditional narratives of what it meant to be a mother; Lynne came face to face with the limits of these narratives when she understood that her infertility would prevent her from giving birth. The adoption of two beautiful sons, and the death of her mother, completed this liberation.

Malissa Smith wrote the first comprehensive narrative about female boxing, titled "A History of Women's Boxing." She is a co-host of the boxing podcast, The WAAR Room, a founding board member of the International Women's Boxing Hall of Fame, and a juror for the weekly Ring Magazine boxing rankings. Malissa's journey into the world of boxing began when she, as a woman in her 40s, summoned the courage to step into a boxing gym and start her training as an amateur.

Caroline de Posada witnessed the power of human transformation while managing the career of her father, global speaker and renowned author Dr. Joachim de Posada. After his death in 2015, Caroline took a leap of faith into uncharted waters. She left her career as a successful attorney and devoted herself to helping others build resilient relationships and define and achieve success. She created a supportive online community called CORE which takes a mind-body approach to physical and emotional wellness. Her mission is to inspire people to live better, follow their dreams and pursue their goals.

THEME 3: PERSONAL TRANSFORMATION

Everything changed for Dr. Tom Garcia when he and his wife invited his good friend John to live with them during the final years of John's life. As he tended to his friend, Tom found himself less and less interested in his practice as a successful chiropractor. He embarked on his exploration of fire rituals and his shamanic self. This is the life Tom lives now.

Mark J. Silverman's life has unfolded in a series of dramatic ups and equally great downs: from homelessness to making a million dollars, to losing it all again. From having a storybook family life to divorce and facing his addictions, Mark's life has been a long and extended ride into more profound and fully knowing self-love.

Co-editor Achim Nowak was handed a "you have a couple of years to live" prognosis in 1988 when he tested HIV-positive. This prognosis took him to an esoteric healing center deep in the Arizona desert where he made contact with spirit and entered an archetypal dark night of soul. When he emerged from his dark night, he left Manhattan for a small Caribbean island where he became a windsurfer. Nothing would ever be the same again.

OUR INVITATION

Enjoy the honest, rich, and captivating stories you're about to read. Savor the broad tapestry of human experience that unfolds in these pages. As you engage with each author, you will understand that the losses, the struggles, and the difficult moments are unexpected paths to hope, possibility and the common beat of life. They are, indeed, the seeds of deep and lasting personal transformation.

In gratitude for traveling and exploring with us,

– Achim Nowak and Rosemary Ravinal

Essays on Loss

Rage Against the Dying of the Light

Carl Ficks, Jr.

The personal losses in Carl Ficks, Jr.'s life started to pile up after more than three decades of work as a successful trial attorney. Then came one more loss; this time, one he chose: Carl said goodbye to his lawyer life and embarked on an entirely new and entirely unrelated career.

Danish author Isak Dinesen once said, "All sorrows can be borne if you tell a story about them." I hope the stories that I share inspire you, regardless of age or obstacle, to never stop moving, learning, experimenting, exploring, or living. These are my sorrows, not unlike those experienced by many and thus not unique. They are simply ones I have embraced and repurposed as the catalyst to step into, and onto, a new stage.

DUST IN THE WIND

I couldn't forget one of our last journeys together.

We were on top of Table Mountain, 12,688 feet above sea level in the Weminuche Wilderness, 500,000 acres of pristine land in Colorado. Staring slack-jawed at a herd of elk in a valley below. Paul had guided me up the Highline Trail to this point on a spotless July day. There we soaked in unobstructed 360-degree views that stretched for 90 miles, drinking the silence and bathing in the brilliance of quiet.

Ruggedly handsome, stealthily intense, and wryly funny, Paul, one of my wife's brothers, had fled a very prominent and public third-generation family business in his early 40s and moved west, first to Arizona and then to Colorado. He reminded me of the legendary mountain man Jeremiah Johnson. Offices and buildings adorned with Paul's famous surname could not harness his spirit or contain his wanderlust. When Paul escaped his nine-to-five corporate prison, he came alive for the first time.

Before our trip, I'd never spent a night in the wild, but that was of no matter for Paul. He scoffed and told me that I was *in shape* and had the *right attitude*. When we met at the Durango airport the day before we set off, Paul mentioned that he'd packed my 50 pounds of gear. After I thanked him, he sternly told me to unpack the gear and repack it myself. "Why?" I asked. So I would know the contents of my pack should we encounter *difficulties*, as he put it. Paul's wilderness skills were unmatched, and the subtle unpack/repack flex was not lost upon me, his pupil for the journey.

He had invited me into one of his many cathedrals in the sky, places where he routinely found peace in good times and solace in turbulent ones. Places where he could, as Jimi Hendrix sang, *kiss the sky*. Here he was his happiest self because he was usually alone. As the husband in Tolstoy's novella *Family Happiness* says, "It's a bad thing not to be able to stand solitude." Paul loved his solitude, which he was graciously about to share with me.

Paul and I geared and gunned up, then trekked into the Weminuche with no watches, no phones, no technology; no contact with, or access to, the outside world. We hiked all day, made camp, then repeated the sequence the next morning. All without *difficulties*. This was the first time I had really, truly kissed the sky.

We emerged three days later and headed into the little mining town of Creede, where we greedily devoured bison burgers and downed a few cold beers at Kip's Grill.

Author and social commentator Jack London is said to have observed that he would rather be a meteor than a sleepy and permanent planet. He believed that man's true purpose in life is to live, not to waste time merely sustaining himself.

Paul was the brightest of meteors, rejecting both the mere sustenance offered by corporate America and the familial yoke to find his true purpose as a runner, high-altitude mountaineer, hunter, fisherman, and all-around badass.

Paul lived, *until he didn't.*

In late February 2014, Paul disappeared without a trace in Arizona. He was 57 years old. A massive search and rescue mission ensued, involving law enforcement helicopters; dogs; and volunteer searchers on foot, horseback, and all-terrain vehicles. The search reached its zenith the second week of March 2014. His name, as if ripped off his old office/prison door, exploded on the front page of a statewide newspaper back east, the *Hartford Courant,* with the ominous headline, "Tomasso Family Member Missing on Arizona Hike."

Missing he was. Paul was dust in the wind.

A DOUBLE WAKE

My mother married young in life, raised three kids, ran the household and worked part-time at a bank. My father firmly believed she had sacrificed her education for the good of maintaining order, and often encouraged her to return to college. But life interfered, and she deferred the quest for a degree.

After my father's passing in 2009, my mother moved purposefully toward achieving her long-deferred goal and enrolled in a local community college. Never one to settle, she pursued her degree in earnest. Her family marveled at the effort and devotion expended by this maternal meteor to earn that diploma.

By the fall of 2013, she had accumulated enough credits to graduate. However, cancer suddenly appeared, seeking to deny my mother the opportunity to walk across the stage with her graduating class in the spring of 2014. Undeterred, my sister magically engineered a ceremony in Mom's hospital room. With "Pomp and Circumstance" filling the hushed silence, the college's President and Dean of Academic Affairs presented my mother with her well-deserved diploma. The Dean, addressing Mom's four captivated grandchildren, said, "She wanted to be an example for you, to show you that with hard work you can achieve anything you want in life." Mom responded that earning her degree at the age of 78 had made a difference in her life.

My mother was a steady presence in my life, *until she wasn't.*

Three short days later, while the search for my brother-in-law Paul continued some 2,500 miles away, her life ended. Like the glowing meteor that she was, my mother died after exhibiting to her grandchildren what it is like to LIVE.

The unbearable sadness of Paul's disappearance muscled in on the unbearable sadness of my mother's passing, both fighting for my attention, energy, and emotional reserves. At my mother's wake, as mourners passed through the line to offer their condolences, they simultaneously asked my wife, Carol, and me, "Any word on Paul?" Carol later said, "I feel like I just did a double wake."

I'm all for two-for-one specials but would rather have them in a bar than a funeral home.

FLATTENED...AGAIN

I handled the two-fer the way I handled most things—by running prodigious amounts of miles. I have competed in road races of all distances, from 5K to the marathon distance of 26.2 miles. Running has been THE common denominator in my life, at once gratifying, cathartic, emotional, exhausting, and dizzyingly fun. While Paul used to worship in nature's high peaks, running was my asphalt cathedral, a place where I routinely found peace in good times and solace in turbulent ones.

The running community never failed to provide a safe harbor, allowing me the space and time to process the peaks and valleys of life. I have literally marked the milestones of my life by running road races. I ran the weekend of my first wedding anniversary; the morning of my first daughter's baptism, four days after 9/11; and the day after the Sandy Hook massacre. Perhaps my most powerful race was the marathon I ran a few weeks after my father died. I yearned for, and required, the nourishment I received at each of those moments, doing what I loved.

Running. Always my saving grace. *Until it wasn't.*

Eight months after the double dose of March doom, I'm flattened by the news. It was the day that time stopped for me. The day my orthopedist uttered the words *hip dysplasia* and issued his mandate: *No more running!*, I drifted, then drifted some more, piling up miles but not via foot. Behind the wheel of my car, I sat on my butt, driving on and on, feeling utterly useless. No more sunrise runs? No more 26.2-mile romps through the Disney parks? No more speedwork at the high school track? No more Thanksgiving runs capped off with a pint of Guinness, or Friday 10-milers?

A throbbing ache enveloped me. Was this the start of the "dying of the light" that the poet Dylan Thomas raged against in *Do Not Go Gentle Into That Good Night*?

THE GRIEF PARADE ROLLS ON

After enduring the trifecta of loss in 2014, I finally regained my footing about six months into 2015. That was when I moved from behind the wheel of my car to the top of a saddle, fully immersing myself in the cycling world. My body propelled me along the asphalt cathedral once again, just in the nick of time.

And then it happened. Again. The grief parade rode into town in September 2015, this time on the occasion of my father-in-law Angelo's sudden death.

I'd had the good fortune of meeting Angelo years before I met his youngest daughter. As a "kid" lawyer in my first firm, I assisted on various legal matters for Angelo's company. He later invited me to one of his son's weddings, where I was introduced to Carol. I would marry her four years later. Angelo and my father were contemporaries and friends, which made my relationship with Angelo deeper and richer. Spending time with him was like hanging out with my dad.

Angelo was awarded a Purple Heart after surviving the Battle of Luzon in WWII, but he could not survive a fall down the stairs in his home, sustained while leaving for work one morning at the age of 90. Here one day and gone the next, much like his son Paul. Angelo was a titan in the construction industry, unfailingly honest and hardworking. His wake lasted over seven hours.

The throbbing ache returned. The continued dying of the light?

IN, OUT, THEN BACK IN

I started practicing law with a small firm in New Britain, Connecticut, in 1988, at the age of 24. My litigation practice grew. As a result, I moved to a significantly larger firm in Hartford, CT, 12 years later. What attracted me to the private practice of law, and especially trial work, were the parallels with the full-contact sports I had loved growing up. Bare-knuckle brawling with your adversaries, the court, and at times, your own clients. Add to that the unrelenting stresses of the practice. There were the Herculean hours; the daily demand to bill every moment of your time; the daily, weekly, monthly, and yearly pressure to build, sustain, and then increase your book of business; the monthly pressure to collect on your invoices; the end-of-year pressure to collect outstanding receivables. Topping it all off, there were the inevitable partner squabbles and the firm's administrative kerfuffles.

After many years, I had to take refuge from the maelstrom. With an open invitation to rejoin the law firm at my convenience, I dipped my toe in the genteel philanthropy pond for a few years, returning to the private practice of law in 2017. Hopeful that the comfort of a law firm I had called home since 2000, and a profession that had served me well since 1988 would reignite the dying light, I dove right back into the cauldron of litigation.

Cauldron or not, I loved it. The camaraderie of the trade. The competitive thrill. A road race, a long bike ride, and hiking in the

Weminuche, all rolled into the single carnival ride known as trial work…and I still get paid handsomely for having this much fun? It was good to be back.

One of my closest friends at the Hartford firm was Dan, a literal and figurative giant in the industry. We would hit the road together for client development junkets and trips to the firm's Washington, DC office. We would attend hearings together in New York City, and tag team at trials. Dan commanded loyalty and respect. He was one of the few at the firm who returned both in kind.

Dan was the paradoxical owner of a menacing, Godfather-esque stare but also a monstrous heart. After my father died, I found a ham, a bag of rolls, and a case of beer buried in my driveway snowbank with a note from Dan reminding me to "Eat and stay hydrated." It was classic Dan.

Upon my return to the firm, Dan and I worked closely on "crumbling foundation" litigation. Homeowners sued their insurance companies for coverage when their foundations, built with defective concrete, began to fall apart. Together we defended the companies. The human toll of this disaster was clearly evident. When I asked one witness about the emotional impact of this calamity, she calmly informed me that she had multiple sclerosis. "Stress is bad for MS," she explained. Another witness, a veteran police officer, quietly wept when I asked him the same question.

Returning to the firm was great, *until it wasn't.*

Was my own foundation crumbling? Was the practice of law taking its toll on me? Was I merely sustaining myself, exactly as Jack London warned against? I peered inside myself from atop the bike saddle and questioned, intensely, what I was doing and why I was doing it. Was I simply moving money from one side of the corporate ledger to the other? Was I positively impacting people's lives?

Critically, was I in service to the community? A commitment to service has been one of my proudest character traits since I was a kid. I delivered the morning paper, seven days a week, for years. A U.S. Postal Service stamp issued in 1952 captures how I felt about my role as a paperboy. Honoring "newspaper boys" for the "important service rendered to their communities and their nation," the stamp further depicts them as standard bearers of "free enterprise." Long before the 24-hour cable news cycle, long before the Internet delivered instant headlines, I delivered the breaking news every morning to my neighbors. I was Walter Cronkite's "mini-me," the print version. This service mindset continued into adulthood.

I struggled to evaluate whether I was staying true to my values. Dylan Thomas's poem was front of mind while this tumultuous internal conflict simmered: "Do not go gentle into that good night,/Old age should burn and rave at close of day;/ Rage, rage against the dying of the light." I was 57 years old, the same age as Paul when he vaporized. I KNEW I had to leave the law before I vaporized, but I felt rudderless, with no idea where to go or what to do.

SUMMONING IT BY THE RIGHT WORD

After a deeply unsatisfying, albeit brief, self-pity party, I hired a coach and started doing some heavy work, channeling my inner alchemist. To put it in cycling terms, the work would have me vacillating between very steep climbs and soaring descents, searching for life's splendor.

Where to start? I picked up the figurative artist's palette in my hand and started to lay and mix my paints. Life experiences. Transferable skills. Attributes. Passions. I swirled the many "life" colors of husband, father, son, paperboy, brother, attorney, endurance athlete, board member, and friend with the *transferable skill* colors of deductive reasoning, leadership, writing, and analytical thinking. I then introduced a few *attribute* colors like perseverance, courage, discipline, grit, and resilience and mixed them with my *passion* paints–service, fitness, wellness.

I was ready to paint the canvas, hopeful that if I "summon[ed] it by the right word, by its right name, it [would] come." Franz Kafka was right when he described the essence of creative magic in these terms. What emerged was a company designed to inspire and motivate people, a company centered around fitness and wellness. A company *in service* to others, helping them thrive.

The euphoria upon finding my "why" was tempered by a gnawing, pyrrhic feeling. I told myself that I was concerned about leaving the steady, generous cash flow and the security found in the legal profession, but I knew this was a subterfuge. What I was *really* deeply concerned about was leaving the firm again, thereby violating the mutual loyalty and respect I so treasured with Dan. A comment Dan had made in early 2021 weighed heavily on me. Notifying me of a bump in my compensation, he had looked me in the eye and said, "Now don't fucking leave the firm again." *Merde!*

PERMISSION GRANTED

Dan usually ended each workday with a "See ya later buddy."

Before heading south for a week with my oldest daughter, Leia, I popped my head into Dan's office to alert him. He said, "OK, see ya later buddy."

Fast forward a few days, when Leia and I would find ourselves in a spin class on the top of the W Hotel in Ft. Lauderdale. I'm pounding miles, watching the sun peek and then rapidly rise over the blue Atlantic. I'm with my college-student daughter... who wants to spend time with her father? I felt like I was back in the Weminuche on Table Mountain, with Bob Marley's song "Give Thanks and Praises" ricocheting in my head.

In the middle of this joyful reverie, I got the news. I would never hear Dan's "See ya later buddy" again. Dan had died in his sleep.

I cycled through the five stages of grief in about 72 hours. And then I cycled, for real, pedaling far, fast, and furiously. Melting the miles, trying to make heads or tails out of the latest loss. I knew that if I ignored the dying of the light I would, like Paul, be dust in the wind.

The sorrowful fog of Dan's death lifted during one emphatic ride the day after his funeral, allowing me to see what his death represented to me: *permission* from my friend. I no longer had to fear letting my friend, my law partner, my comrade down. I had permission to leave the firm. Permission to leave the practice of law. Permission, at the age of 57, to live. To really LIVE.

So I decided to leave.

And I started to live.

VERITAS

The motto for my undergraduate school, Providence College, is *Veritas,* Latin for "truth." My alma mater drove and shaped my intellectual, spiritual, and emotional maturity. An education made possible by my parents' unwavering sacrifices and the generosity of the Dominican Order. An experience which still defines my life. The *Veritas* motto has unfailingly provided my moral compass on decisions and actions large and small, like powering my return to the law firm in 2017 when my then-employer refused to play by the rules.

In order to be "true" to myself, I knew I had to follow *Veritas*. I knew I had to practice what I had repeatedly preached to Leia and my youngest daughter, Sarah. I knew I had to launch the company I had created. I knew I had to "rage against the dying of the light."

The mental toughness coach Chris Dorris defines all-in-ness as an "infinitely committed state." And that's where I am–all in and infinitely committed to a company I call No Surrender, a nod to the Springsteen tune of the same name. I listened to the song incessantly while riding the city bus to campus in Washington, DC. When I wanted to quit law school, the Boss would loop endlessly on my Walkman and tell me not to give up.

So I didn't. And I won't. To date, Paul has never been found, but Veritas saved me from disappearing. Dylan Thomas gave us the example of the "Wild men who caught and sang the sun in flight,/And learn, too late, they grieved it on its way,/Do not go gentle into that good night."

I'm grateful that I did not learn too late. My own experiences with grief have fueled my refusal to go gentle into that good night. Instead, we rage on.

Carl Ficks, Jr. is an endurance athlete and former trial lawyer with a career spanning 30+ years. He works with leaders to increase their effectiveness, and with their teams to boost engagement and productivity.

Finding Your Way Back to Joy

Dr. Betsy Guerra

When her two-year-old daughter died unexpectedly, Dr. Betsy Guerra came face-to-face with excruciating pain and grief. A clinical psychotherapist, author, and speaker, she shares her story of loss vulnerably. In doing so, she teaches others how to use their pain to rise above adversity and find their way to joy and deep spirituality.

It must have been shortly after seven in the morning when the hallway door flew open, revealing my precious two-year-old with her crazed and curly brown hair. Fofi smiled with her entire face, as she usually did, causing me to smile back. "Good morning, princess," I said joyfully as I kneeled and opened my arms to welcome her. She rushed to my embrace, where I covered her up with kisses while she giggled.

We had a pool and BBQ family day planned on this beautiful Sunday. Later that day, Fofi and her big sister were outside helping dad prepare everything, while I took care of the food in the kitchen.

As people started to arrive, Fofi came inside the house to get me. She said, *"Mami, yo quiero estar donde tú estés,"* which translates to, "Mommy, I want to be where you are." That was her way of asking me to go into the pool with her. Fortunately, I did.

We called my husband, Alain, from the pool to join our usual cheerleading game. I carried Fofi on my shoulders, and Daddy carried us on his. Fofi's little but strong hands clutched my head. I imagined it was her way of feeling safe.

After the first cheerleading pose, my oldest daughter, Chichi, joined us. I put Fofi on one of my shoulders and her big sister on the other. Daddy picked us up and placed the three of us on his shoulders. Chichi gave Fofi confidence, so this time she threw her hands up in the air during her cheer performance. Chichi was an amazing big sister, and they were the best of friends. They were so close that it was hard to imagine one without the other.

It was the perfect day.

Until the clock struck five.

WHERE'S FOFI?

I was standing in the pool chatting with my friend, Cristi. Suddenly, she asked, "Where's Fofi?"

Fofi had just been playing with the other kids. She had been right by me. What caused Cristi to ask for Fofi? Something about her question shot fear into my heart. Instantly I became panic-stricken.

I scanned the area at lightning speed.

Where is she?

My chest tightened.

My heart pounded.

I still couldn't find her anywhere. I zoomed in with hypervigilant eyes.

She was right by me.

My gaze shifted down.

She was beside me... but at the bottom of the pool.

There, through the clear, wavering water, I caught a glimpse of my daughter's red and white polka-dot Minnie Mouse bathing suit.

At the bottom of that traitorous body of water lay my precious two-year-old daughter, Fofi.

Immediately, I dove in to grab her. I held my breath as I clutched her body in my arms to rush her to the surface. I struggled to pull us both above the water, pushing against the resistance that tried to keep us down.

I managed to carry her out of the water and laid her on the pavers by the edge of the pool. Foamy water started coming out from her nose or perhaps her mouth. It is hard to remember exactly.

I think I screamed for help. I tried to give her CPR, but I wasn't sure I knew what I was doing. Although there was commotion and hysteria in the background, for me the world stopped. It was just the two of us.

My husband rushed to our side. His eyes projected the fear I felt when I heard Cristi's question. Instinctively, we both knew how terrible this was.

He spoke to Fofi as though there was no one else around. "You are strong, my love," he said with a tone of hopeful desperation while holding her lifeless body in his arms. "Stay with me. You can do this. Look at Daddy," he commanded as he moved her shoulders, trying to get a reaction from her. He spoke to her, kissed her, and repeatedly brought her face toward his heart in an embrace.

I experienced what happened next as if I were watching my life unravel in a movie. I silently wailed in desperation, witnessing each second pass in slow motion. My thoughts echoed over and over: *This is not happening; This can't be true.*

I felt compelled to pray.

I am a woman of faith. I believe in a God of love and mercy that I knew would save my daughter, and I couldn't waste a minute on fear. *Please save her, my dear Lord. Save my little girl.* I made big promises in exchange for His mercy. I felt peace amidst the terror because I was so sure He would listen to my supplication.

My neighbor approached me as I paced back and forth near our kids' trampoline. "Have faith, my love," Gladys whispered as she hugged me.

"I know that God will save her," I responded confidently. Gladys squeezed me tighter and then gave me the space to turn around and continue praying alone. *Please save her, Dear God. I'm raising her for you. Let me finish my job. Please save my little girl.*

Minutes later, the paramedics arrived. They worked on my sleeping beauty and moved her unresponsive body to the ambulance. Someone brought me dry clothes to put on over my wet bathing suit, and I pulled them on hurriedly.

I still remember the chilling air that pierced through my bones as we sat in the front seat of that air-conditioned ambulance.

My entire body was shaking. Alain noticed and embraced me to help contain the shivering. The ambulance driver was kind and reassuring, though I don't remember his face or his words. Everything was a blur, including the siren that was blaring, somewhere in the background—or so it seemed. It must have been just above us.

MAKE HER HEART BEAT!

Within five minutes, we arrived at Baptist Hospital. They took us to the emergency room immediately. The room felt small and crowded by the medical staff taking care of our little girl. The doctors spoke in quick commands and responses. Their focus was on Fofi. I could see how much they cared about her. I trusted them.

Be her doctor, Dear God. Save her through them, I prayed. *Give them the wisdom to do whatever is needed. Please save her!*

The doctors tried urgently to save her. I can't recall the details because the moment was chaotic and surreal. The only thing real was the pain. I can still feel it as I revisit the scene to write these words for you.

There was a monitor by the right side of her stretcher where my husband and I stood. I didn't know how to interpret the data it showed, but I did notice a straight line. Was that *the* flat line?

Make her heart beat! Make her heart beat! Make her heart beat! I begged God with unwavering faith. I've always felt that we need to be specific when we pray, and that's what I did at that moment, to the best of my abilities.

My brain was drained and paralyzed, but it felt too risky to stop praying. I had to let God know that I believed. I asked Him to give me a phrase or scripture I could repeat in prayer without having to think.

I can do all things through Christ who strengthens me. (Philippians 4:13)

No! I rejected that scripture because it suggested that I could endure whatever came next. It suggested that Fofi wouldn't make it. I figured it was my fear and hopelessness bringing it to me. I knew God would save her. He had to! He loved me and He knew I loved Him. *Be her doctor, dear God. Save my little girl. Make her heart beat.*

Suddenly, amidst the turmoil, I heard an inner voice say, *You know Fofi could be saved and not be the Fofi you knew.* I thought about my oldest sister, who was born healthy but contracted rubella when she was nine months old. The high fever from the disease created complications and put her in a coma. She almost died, but *God made her heart beat.*

The inner voice continued, *What if He made Fofi's heart beat, but she stopped being the sweet, jolly, funny girl we knew? What if her heart beats, but her brain dies? What if...?*

My mind was quick to react. *I don't care! She's my daughter. I'll love her regardless. Let her heart beat, God. Please don't take her. Make her heart beat!*

Minutes that seemed eternal, yet not long enough, passed by. The medical staff continued fighting for her life. My husband positioned himself closer to her peaceful face and urged, "Come on, Fofi. You are strong. Wake up. We're going to watch a movie tonight. You've got this!"

My heart was crushed. I'm not sure which pain was more excruciating—the one that came from the possibility of losing my daughter or the one caused by witnessing my husband's pain and desperation. I was powerless. I couldn't do anything to save my Fofi's life, nor could I mend the pieces of Alain's broken heart.

GOD'S WILL

All I could do was pray...so I did. Incessantly. *Save my Fofi, dear Lord. Make her heart beat. Be her doctor. Use the medical staff as your vessel. Show them the way to bring my princess to life.* I repeated my prayers over and over again. Then I added, reluctantly, *Let your will be done.*

Suddenly my prayer became a song. I didn't plan for it. I don't know how it happened. I just know that my knees buckled and I found myself kneeling by the stretcher, singing *Cántico Celeste* (Heavenly Chant). It was a song of hope that I often sang for my girls as a lullaby. Its lyrics reassured me that the night and its dread would pass, that soon the sun would light up my heart.

At that moment, I knew God's will was different from mine. The pain was so unbearable, I disconnected from my senses. I left my body as I did by the pool moments earlier. The movie I didn't want to watch continued to unspool before me.

Everything was happening fast, but in slow motion. The loud turmoil was mute. I knew the medical staff were talking, but I couldn't understand what they were saying. Then their faces screamed what we were not ready to hear. Their droopy, sad eyes and disheartened spirits conveyed that there was nothing else they could do. They must have said, "I'm sorry," or something like that. I watched as, one by one, they lowered their gaze to the floor and slowly left the room.

The monitor still showed a straight line. *The* flat line.

God didn't make my daughter's heart beat.

I felt my own heart flatlining as the medical staff exited the room in slow motion, leaving my daughter's lifeless body behind. I wanted to scream, but I had no voice. I wanted to wake up, but I was not sleeping. I wanted to die, but my heart kept beating.

It was surreal.

The pain I felt was numbed by disbelief. My thoughts raced. *This can't be happening. How will I live without her? I can't do this. I want to die too. Take me with you, Fofi. How am I going to tell your older sister that she'll never see her best friend again? God, take me too!*

I fell out of touch with my senses once again. It was as if I could see myself from afar. My body was on autopilot. I was breathing because my subconscious made me. I stood because my legs were in the habit of doing so. My body was just—there.

Someone from the medical staff stepped in to alert us that it was time to say goodbye to Fofi. *He wants me to leave my daughter? How can I go home without her?* I couldn't understand what was happening. I felt so lost. *This can't be happening! This can't be!* My brain screamed in silence.

My husband and I wanted to be there until the last second. I knew all too well that the body lying on the stretcher was just the shell of my precious daughter, but that was the very flesh I had embraced, caressed, bathed, and held daily for two years, eight months, and 19 days. That was the body I gave birth to and loved into existence. Through her very eyes, I had seen rays of light and joy. From those lips, I had witnessed countless smiles and felt a thousand kisses. The little hands that lay still now had once held mine or surrounded my neck in a hug.

It was *all* dead—her body, her kisses, her smiles, her hugs—they were all gone.

MY LIFE ENDED THAT DAY

My life, as I knew it, ended that day.

At bedtime, I lay next to my husband in silence, with my heavy eyes open. A part of me wanted to pause time so it would always be the last day I saw Fofi. The other part wanted to fast forward so I could die too and spare my soul from the pain. Minutes or hours later, my eyes and mind finally gave in and shut down.

The next thing I remember is being on the floor of my daughter's bathroom, rocking back and forth in the fetal position. I vividly recall clawing at my hair in a desperate and futile attempt to get rid of my thoughts and flashbacks. They were unbearable. I kept replaying the nightmare by the pool. I was trying to make sense of what had occurred. I didn't understand.

I felt guilt, pain, disbelief, terror, anger, frustration, confusion, and excruciating pain. These emotions haunted me all at once. For the first time in my life, I understood why people "go crazy." That was the moment of deepest despair and hopeless darkness I had experienced in my life. I couldn't fall asleep again and staying awake was unbearable. I was trapped by monsters that tortured my brain. I thought I had hit rock bottom hours before, but rock bottom was even deeper now. I wanted my life to end so I wouldn't have to feel.

But my heart kept beating.

I soon learned that life after loss is deeply painful.

I cried daily for months and lost my joy for quite a while. Every bone in my body hurt as the cancer of grief metastasized.

Hopelessness threatened my peace, but I didn't let it triumph. I was going to be happy again. I was determined to find my way to healing and joy.

And I did.

I ROSE UP.

F.A.I.T.H. IS MY SUPERPOWER

As I looked back to understand what helped me go from **Hurt** to **Hope** to **Happy**, I realized I have a superpower. It's called FAITH.

The Bible says "... faith is the assurance of things hoped for, the conviction of things not seen." (Hebrews 11:1)

Faith is trusting that you can be happy again, even if you're suffering right now. It is being confident that your pain will eventually liberate you, not condemn you. Faith allows you to have hope for a better version of your life, no matter how impossible it may seem at the moment.

F.A.I.T.H. is also an acronym that describes the set of tools I used to rise above my pain.

Fertilizing pain
Acceptance
Interpretation
Team
Habits

These are the secret components to build a life full of hope and healing.

Regardless of the nature of your pain, F.A.I.T.H. can elevate you to the highest, most joyous version of yourself.

Fertilizing pain

Start by viewing and embracing pain as a FERTILIZER. Fertilizers are made of horse manure. Pain feels and stinks like poop, too. But fertilizers also nourish plants, help them grow and give fruit. The same is true for grief. Pain humbles you, builds resilience, develops empathy, brings perspective, strengthens you, and helps you become a higher version of yourself.

Acceptance

Embracing pain as the path to healing gave me hope when heartache felt excruciating. It helped me respond to unexpected and undesirable life events in a more graceful manner. I still feel the discomfort and sting when things don't go my way, but I trust that they are training me for something bigger. Besides, I know I can do hard things. This attitude helps me pursue radical ACCEPTANCE.

Interpretation

After acceptance, the time is right to examine your INTERPRETATION and reframe it into one that helps you regain peace.

Life is neutral. We are the ones who interpret it in a positive or negative manner. Therefore, we have the power to determine how to feel about life by changing our interpretation. We own our worldview and, hence, the emotions that our outlook brings forth in us.

Reframing—changing the perspective with which you look at a situation—is hard. Not reframing, however, is much harder in the long term. It is detrimental to stay with your unquestioned paradigms and unchallenged assumptions that you are not resilient enough to rise from adversity.

Team

When I have a hard time practicing acceptance and changing my perspective into a more positive one, I reach out to someone in my TEAM. I have great friends and mentors who shine their wisdom when I feel stuck.

Choosing an All-Star team to support you will help you bounce back from painful experiences. It will help you grow and thrive. To surround yourself with people who are aligned with your values and desired outcome is to set yourself up for success.

Create a team of friends, family members, mentors, and professionals who have the empathy and wisdom you need. Include people who inspire hope, lift you up, and are a step ahead in a similar journey. You don't even have to know them personally!

Habits

Those people will guide you and give you hope when your pain feels greater than you can bear. They will also push you and hold you accountable for engaging in beneficial HABITS. These habits will equip you with an extra layer of protection that replenishes your *adaptation energy*, which is your ability to cope with daily stressors.

Healthy habits—such as mindful eating, exercising, meditating, praying, sleeping, and thinking positively—provide the strength you need to carry on. Because you don't have to think about what you do automatically, habits give rest to your mind and allow you to function with minimal effort.

F.A.I.T.H. truly gives us a powerful set of tools, but it is only effective if we practice it with *faith*. We must believe in the process, in our ability to do the impossible, in the people who guide us, and in a higher power that will help us through it. May you live and rise in faith!

Dr. Betsy Guerra is a bilingual psychotherapist, international speaker, and author of *Hurt 2 Hope: Heal the Pain of Loss, Grief, and Adversity*. She is the founder of Better with Betsy, a psycho-spiritual approach to supporting individuals and elevating humanity.

The Return to a Homeland That Wasn't

Rosemary Ravinal

Cuban-born Rosemary Ravinal has been haunted by thoughts of life in Cuba and a cultural bereavement which she cannot reconcile. Life in the United States made the difference in what she became, yet the desire for Cuban identity remains.

Scanning my brain for the pivotal moments and the people who made an indelible difference in my life, I conjured up an array of topics that ended as discarded drafts. The value of any one dramatic moment in my 68-year timeline evaporated away once I began to explore it on the page. None commanded the gravitas of a real turning point.

I could not land on a compelling difference-making event until, in a fit of insomnia, I picked up a book and had an epiphany. *Ninety Miles and a Lifetime Away: Memories of Early Cuban Exiles,* by David Powell, had lain unfinished for weeks on my nightstand. And voilà, there it was—the life-altering event that had uprooted me from my homeland abruptly at age seven and brought me to a strange new world.

Many of the accounts in Powell's book mirrored mine. Others diverged because of the circumstances that brought the authors to this country. Some spoke of a deepened sense of *cubanidad* after they visited Cuba as adults. Others, like me, had never returned.

WE NEVER EXPECTED TO STAY

My parents and I arrived in the United States on July 23, 1962. We shared the tragedy of thousands of Cubans whose lives were upended quickly and dramatically by political revolution. We brought with us the hope that the separation from our homeland would be short-lived, given the political instability that had characterized life in Cuba for much of the 20th century. We never expected that the communist takeover would bedevil the island for over 60 years and make our permanent return impossible.

What would have happened had my parents decided to stay and succumb to the mandatory indoctrination and totalitarian policies of the Cuban revolution? This is a question asked by thousands of Cubans like me who were brought to the U.S. as children in the first wave of migration. Some young refugees came unaccompanied in a clandestine exodus called Operation Pedro Pan. Their parents feared that Castro and the Communist Party were planning to terminate parental rights and place minors in reeducation centers. The transplanted children lived in camps and foster homes in South Florida and elsewhere for years.

NOSTALGIA AND VIVID MEMORIES

Unlike the Pedro Pan generation, I was fortunate to emigrate with my mother and father. My gratitude for the opportunities and privileges I have enjoyed in the U.S. is boundless. Yet, with the passing of time comes a nagging sense of loss of family, tradition, national identity, and an idealized way of life. Curiously, these *añoranzas* or bouts of nostalgia come with surprisingly vivid memories I give myself permission to savor.

My parents' decision to leave Cuba with their only daughter, a five-dollar bill, and merely the clothes we were wearing made the profound difference in what I would become. Their decision to live in New York and not settle in Miami, the burgeoning Cuban exile mecca where friends and former neighbors would try to reconstitute the lives they left behind; their decision to enroll me in Catholic boarding school for the first years of my new life when I had never been away from home; these choices created lasting trauma that followed me to adulthood. As I grow older, I try to imagine what my life would have been like had we not left Cuba.

GO TO PRISON OR LEAVE

The big changes in my young life began in 1961. Fidel Castro's revolution had swept the island two years earlier and by now his intention to turn Cuba into a communist state was evident in every facet of life. Private enterprises and foreign companies were seized, and their local employees were forced to do hard labor in the sugarcane fields or join the military. Catholic schools were shuttered, and public schools were obligated to teach revisionist history and the doctrine of the nascent revolutionary government.

My father worked in finance for the Coca-Cola Bottling Company. My mother was an elementary school teacher. Both lost their jobs and refused to be complicit with the demands of the revolution.

That meant leaving the country or risking prison. The choice was clear. But leaving Cuba was fraught with countless material and emotional hurdles. Plane tickets had to be purchased in U.S. dollars. There was a long waiting list for flights, and after 1961, people were not allowed to leave with anything more than five dollars and thirty pounds of luggage each. Permission for entry into the United States required a resident sponsor. Fortunately, my mother's older sister was a U.S. citizen living in New York City. We lived with her until we could get on our feet.

Cubans who had decided to leave were considered traitors to the revolution and repudiated publicly. We were called *gusanos,* or worms, by neighbors who turned on us for their self-preservation. We could not leave the house without some type of shaming incident. My friends refused to play with me. The two boys who lived next door scornfully pelted me with oranges if they saw me in the courtyard. One incident left a purple bruise under my eye and forced me to stay indoors indefinitely.

Neighborhood spies watched the house to track people and any items going in or out. We would have to forfeit the house an uncle built for us and all its contents. But in the middle of the night, I remember large parcels being hauled surreptitiously over the wall that separated the back of our house from the alley, destined for the home of a relative. Sadly, my piano was too big to carry to the other side.

THE DAY OF DEPARTURE, AND THE FISHBOWL

The day of departure remains etched in my memory. People in olive uniforms, matching caps, heavy boots, and guns in their holsters entered through the front door and marched down the hallways of our house taking inventory. We were ushered out with our three suitcases. I held my favorite doll, Rosita, dressed in her finest outfit, tight to my chest.

The trip to Havana airport was long and hot. I sat on my mother's lap with my head out the window. She told me to look carefully and say goodbye to all the buildings, the trees, and flowers because I would not see them again for a long time.

The airport appeared massive and buzzing with activity. I had never seen an airplane on the ground before. After saying goodbye to aunts, uncles, and cousins, we had to wait in a glass-enclosed room dubbed the *pecera,* or fishbowl. From inside, we could see our family on the other side, pushing up against the glass, crying and sending air kisses. I remember that people everywhere were crying. At one point, my mother put on sunglasses to hide her puffy, red eyes. I cried, too, because the scene was so sad that even grown men were crying. Maybe millions of tears were the water in the fishbowl, I thought.

I clutched Rosita in one hand and my mother's hand in the other as we approached the *milicianos,* stone-faced people dressed in the same olive-green military uniforms as the ones who took over our house, standing behind a long table. An enormous portrait of Fidel hung behind them. The officials told us to take off all our jewelry and empty our suitcases. They rifled through our belongings and tore up family photos and my mother's college diploma. My father's watch, my parents' wedding bands, and my mother's prized ruby engagement ring were confiscated. The officials even searched the diaper of a baby in the arms of a woman standing behind us.

When it was my turn to be searched, a man with thick stubby fingers took my gold name bracelet. I wondered innocently if he had a daughter named Rosa Maria, too. Luckily, he did not notice the small diamond studs on my ears. (I still have them.) Another man yanked Rosita from my hands, took off her clothes, and carefully inspected her body. He shook her like a rattle, listening for anything stashed inside. Then, another man grabbed her head, ripped it off her body and took a closer look. Disappointed, he returned the mangled doll to me in pieces.

Decades later my mother would tell me about the humiliation of having to disrobe and have her private parts probed by a matron who was looking for hidden valuables.

When we boarded the Pan American plane you could hear people crying. No one said a word. My mother gave me the window seat and told me to check the seat pocket in front for chewing gum. I found none.

People applauded when the plane took off. My parents just sat looking somber. I asked my father to fix Rosita, but she was so damaged that he could not put her back together. He said it was better to leave her on the plane so she could return to Cuba and be taken to the doll cemetery. I would later understand that the headless Rosita would be a lasting reminder of that traumatic day.

COLD, COLD, AND MORE COLD

Life in the U.S. was cold, followed by more of the cold, and then some more. The Caribbean breezes of Cuba were replaced by blistering wind and blizzards that nearly froze my fingers off. The cheerful and warm classroom of my Catholic school fourth-grade classroom was history. Instead, I trembled in the drafty halls and ice-cold floors of St. Joseph's boarding school for girls.

The loving company of friends, family, and neighbors in Camagüey was replaced by classmates who did not speak Spanish and by long stretches of solitude because they shunned "the foreign girl." I missed the smell of tobacco that grew on my grandfather's farm. And the crystal sand of Varadero Beach where the water was so clear that I could see my toes no matter how deep I went.

A BUSTLING CAREER AND MUTED IDENTITY

As my life evolved and the political climate in Cuba became implacable, my interest in going back waned. An adrenaline-packed career in public relations and media, three marriages and three divorces, and one extraordinary daughter kept my thoughts focused elsewhere. While living and working among New York's Hispanic elite, my sense of Cuban identity was muted by the mix of nationalities in a city where Puerto Ricans and Dominicans outnumbered Cubans. During my 30s and 40s, I felt a widening sense of displacement. I belonged to many communities and to none. I married a Cuban journalist to reconnect with my roots, but that union was short-lived.

HOW DIFFERENT WOULD IT HAVE BEEN?

Occasionally, I wondered how my life would have turned out had I stayed and grown up in Cuba. How *different* would it have been? My only references were the portrayals of contemporary Cuban women in books, theater, feature films, documentaries, and news reports. They invariably fell into a few roles. They were revolutionary feminists, or beleaguered housewives struggling to stretch the ration card to feed their families, or possibly doctors and scientists who eked out a living as escorts for tourists. Social media and accounts from distant relatives filled in the gaps in my perceptions.

Ninety miles and close to six decades separated me from my homeland. The difference could not have been more dramatic. I wanted to find out for myself what I had left behind.

THE RIGHT TIME TO GO BACK THAT WASN'T

My curiosity was piqued when in 2015 President Barack Obama extended an olive branch to Cuban leaders and re-established diplomatic relations after half a century of severed ties. It seemed like the right time to go back. Thousands of tourists were visiting from all over the world, which gave me a measure of comfort that I would not be arrested for uttering anything against the revolution in public. There were flights to most major Cuban cities, including my hometown. My cousins who had remained on the island were ecstatic at the prospect of receiving me. They were saving their rations to make me a special welcome meal.

It was November 2, 2016, and I was scheduled to depart on my birthday, November 9. My bags were overflowing with socks, underwear, soap, medicines, and other items in short supply or virtually nonexistent in Cuba. Among my parcels would be an urn with my father's ashes destined for the farmhouse where he was born. November 2 was my father's birthday; he had passed three months earlier. As I turned to face the urn on the bookcase to say happy birthday, I tripped on one of the bags, fell hard on the marble floor, and fractured my pelvis.

The injury would sideline me for three months. The long-awaited trip was postponed until February of 2017, but by then Donald Trump had reversed Obama's policy of rapprochement. Travel to Cuba became risky again.

The trip would have bookended my life by returning me to my roots at age 60. If I had gone, would it have made a difference in my sense of Cuban identity? I would love to compare my experience in the diaspora to the lessons I would learn from revisiting the sounds, smells, and sights of daily life in my native country.

By my 70th birthday, I may yet touch the earth of my birth again.

Rosemary Ravinal built a career as a TV host, news commentator, spokesperson, and corporate communications leader before becoming a bilingual public speaker and executive speaker coach. Since 2000, she has lived in South Florida, center of the Cuban diaspora.

Reflections on Loss

Those who get stuck in the pain of loss are often blocked from finding joy, living their best lives, and serving the world. Suffering, if unquestioned, can "leave a hole in the fabric of one's existence," according to wisdom teacher Eckhart Tolle. But "when you go deep enough into the formless, the dreadful is no longer dreadful, it is sacred," he observes.

Three essays in this anthology, including my own, shed light on different expressions of loss and demonstrate how finding the sacred dimension to the pain brings us closer to our essence. Each essay lays bare a perception of impermanence and grief that millions of humans have experienced. Loss of beloved family members, loss of a career, loss of physical abilities, and loss of a homeland and cultural identity are the themes in this section. These highly personal narratives show us that what we lose can lead us to connecting with all of who we really are.

DON'T LET YOUR LIGHT DIE

Loss showed up in many forms in Carl Ficks, Jr.'s life. The disappearance of one of his favorite brothers-in-law was followed by the loss of other towering individuals in his life—his mom, his father-in-law, his law partner and mentor, Dan. A loss of Carl's running prowess, and a loss of his passion for work that had nurtured him for a very long time.

It would have been tempting to fold and get lost in sorrow. But no, Carl defiantly challenges us. Notice the dying of your light and know that there is a path forward.

Carl's guidance is refreshingly practical and no-nonsense. "Pity parties are a waste of time and energy," Carl asserts. "You have many transferable skills—they are just lying in wait. In lieu of having a pity party, grab your palette and start mixing your colors. If you summon them by the right word, by their right name, they will come. Like my mother earning her college degree at 78 years old."

Mixing his colors began with Carl's willingness to follow his Veritas—his truth—as he noticed the dying of his light. He urges us to do the same: "Follow your Veritas. 'Likes' and 'followers' on social media are overrated. Engagement is key. Engage with, and be in service to, others. And cash flow is useless if you are wallowing in angst. If you don't like the reflection in the mirror, then you're not on the Veritas train."

Loss is often a wake-up call to face deeper truths about ourselves and our life. Consider loss an invitation to do just that. Go on and board the train.

CHANGE YOUR INTERPRETATION OF EVENTS

When Dr. Betsy Guerra's precious two-year-old daughter drowned in the family pool, Betsy came face-to-face with excruciating pain and grief. Her life as she knew it ended that day. Her deep faith in God transformed her. She embraced her suffering as the path to healing, even when the heartache was unbearable, and emerged a resolute guide for others navigating their own losses.

Her loss forced Betsy to rigorously question every aspect of her faith and religious beliefs. The power of this self-reflection informs Betsy's mission to create supportive communities of family, mentors and professionals with collective wisdom and deep empathy for people in mourning. It also inspired Betsy to claim the word F.A.I.T.H. as an acronym for the tools that help us forward after loss.

F = Fertilizing Pain; A = Acceptance; I = Interpretation; T = Team; H = Habits.

"Embracing pain as the path to healing gave me hope when heartache felt excruciating," explains Betsy. "It helped me respond to unexpected and undesirable life events in a more graceful manner."

Embracing her pain also led Betsy to radical acceptance. Radical acceptance is a choice that we all can make, every moment of every day. As Betsy shares: "When something out of my control is robbing me of my peace, I recite internally, *I fully accept this situation exactly how it is.* Radical acceptance invites you to surrender fully to the *as is* nature of life and cease trying to bend reality. In doing so, you are freed from the suffering caused by resistance. You then have the power to invest all your energy on overcoming adversity and fulfilling your life's purpose."

A critical precondition for finding our life's purpose is the willingness to examine our interpretation of what occurred and, if necessary, reframe this interpretation. "When I first lost my daughter," Betsy elaborates, "my interpretation of her death went something like this: 'She was too young... She was supposed to bury ME... I can't live without her... I will never be happy again...' These thoughts informed the identity I adopted as *the grieving mother who lost a child.*"

Betsy understood that holding on to this interpretation would not serve her. "That role didn't fit the bigger plans God had for me, so I decided to change my interpretation into: 'I am the

<u>chosen</u> mother of an angel.' Because the subconscious mind believes whatever you tell it, I soon became the kind of person who feels blessed to have a child in heaven, thinks she's a VIP in the Kingdom, and is eternally grateful for the lessons that came with loss. I no longer miss my precious daughter because I continue to love and feel her spiritually every day of my life."

If you wish to chart a purpose-driven life after loss, accept that some inner homework is in store. Do the work. Make F.A.I.T.H. your friend. And don't go it alone.

OWN YOUR PERSONAL NARRATIVE

My story probes the life-altering loss of my homeland following the communist coup and revolution in Cuba. As a seven-year-old only child, I had no idea how the displacement would make an indelible difference in my world view.

Six decades later, I have learned that ruminations on the past should serve only to illuminate your present and future. Looking back and wondering "what if I had been raised in Cuba" only deepens the sadness that comes from being uprooted.

I confess—I would love to compare my experience in the diaspora to the lessons I would learn from the sounds, smells, and sights of daily life in my native country. Yet, I know that every minute spent wishing I had lived a different life is a minute spent wasting my own.

I have learned that our heritage and cultural history help us understand ourselves but do not define us. Our personal narratives matter regardless of where we come from. I invite you to collect your memories and experiences—the happy and the sad ones—and tell your story in your own voice so they are never forgotten.

Like waves on the ocean, moments crest and vanish. That is why it is important to chronicle the ups and downs, the losses and triumphs, so we can all grow together.

Our individual and combined histories are an indispensable collection of narratives that help us make sense of the world as it is today. Be radically curious about where you came from and the humans who preceded you. And share those stories with heart and honesty to create better paths for society.

– Rosemary Ravinal

Essays on Courage

Unveiling My Authentic Self

Alisa Sample-Alexander

Motivational speaker, recording artist and learning professional Alisa Sample-Alexander had neatly divided her life into separate versions of herself. As she felt increasingly constrained by these divisions, it took a moment of courage and inspiration in front of over a thousand people for Alisa to shatter her own inner glass ceiling and step into a more authentic version of herself.

I've had a blessed life, truly. You might even say I've had two blessed lives. That's because for a long time I led two separate lives, drawing on two separate selves: my motivational speaker self, and my musical, artistic self. And both lives were wonderful, for many years.

Here is a highlight from the life of my motivational speaker self:

I'm in South Africa, at the time when Nelson Mandela is president. In my role as a facilitator, I stand before a group of learners. My students, of various ethnicities, have never experienced such a phenomenon: The leader in the room is not only a brown person, but a woman. This is revolutionary. I bravely nudge groups of Black, White, and Indian South Africans to "mix it up" and sit together and learn together. I teach those who worked for the police in the former government, helping to enforce and uphold apartheid, alongside those who had suffered from that racist system. I teach with such passion and professionalism that workers who keep the grounds—people who look like me, a very brown-skinned individual—bring their children just to sit in the back of the room to watch me as I guide the learning experience. They want their children to catch a glimpse of the future, to see for themselves what is possible when given a fair chance.

I'll never forget my students in South Africa and how grateful I felt to be using my gifts as a teacher. Yes, I have been blessed.

In my second life as a singer, there were more blessings. Here is a literal high point from the life of my artistic self:

I'm onstage on a mountain in Kenya, leading a song in Swahili with hundreds of singers eager to share their gift. We face an audience of tens of thousands. Imagine standing on a mountain and as far as you can see in every direction there are people hungry for faith, hungry for change, and hungry to be inspired. The excitement in the air alone makes you catch your breath and know for certain that something life-changing is about to happen. There are believers who have traveled for days just to be in a space of faith. There are people on the ground, sitting and standing in the trees, and even a crowd out of view on the opposite side of the mountain. An overflow of believers who will only be able to experience the evening through what they feel, not through what they can see.

I'll never forget what I saw and how grateful I felt to be using my gifts as a singer on that stage.

In all honesty, these moments and so many others that have come and gone have made me almost feel guilty for wanting more. And yet…

IS THIS REALLY ALL THERE IS?

Years ago, after so many wonderful personal and professional experiences, I had this moment in my life where I felt I plateaued, like I'd hit a wall and thought perhaps my greatest days were behind me. A series of deaths of those I loved dearly, failed love relationships, friends that turned into frenemies, and a career that seemed to have stalled became my new reality. I was spending more time daydreaming than living my dreams.

Like many, I searched for the secret key to the door that led to the next level of achievement. It seemed to be available to some, but so elusive to me. Like many, I felt that deep ache knowing that I could be better–be *more*– if I could just figure out how. Was there a book with all the answers? A sensei who could unlock it all? A secret handshake? A password even? Despite an amazing life and successes that I was grateful for, it seemed that I had reached a point where instead of living, breathing, and moving full out, my gifts were minimized or sidelined.

But I knew there was more. There was more inside me wanting to share, wanting to give, and wanting a seat at the table.

There had to be more big, amazing moments ahead of me.

I felt unfulfilled and I also felt angry. My spiritual teachers and mentors seemed to have it all together. I examined their lives and studied their stories. Every sermon ended in faith for better and hope for the future. Every mentor lesson ended with a quippy-sounding *Keep the faith, I believe in you*, or a *You can do it* that didn't seem to address the realities and complexities I was experiencing. I wanted to scream back, "I hear you, but it's just so much more complicated than that!"

Some of those who inspired me had life storylines like mine, and I knew I still had plenty to learn from them. I was most certain of one thing: I knew I didn't know. As opposed to walking around emotionally blind and clueless, not knowing that I didn't know, at least I could say this: I had gone to the classes, attended the church services, read the books, studied the history, and sat at the feet of giants, but I was still stuck.

What exactly had happened to me? I'd been blessed with a middle-class upbringing and private school education, and wonderful parents. In some ways, I think my background gave me the impression that having advantages in some areas would mean having advantages in all.

My parents are phenomenal people who despite great, great hardships rose above more obstacles than I'll ever see. My mother is pictured in her primary school pictures without shoes. My father never finished a full year of school for helping his family make extra money by picking cotton and fruit with migrant farm workers up and down Texas freeways. Despite poverty, segregation and the cruelties of Jim Crow, they both graduated from their respective high schools as valedictorians and went on to have advanced degrees and prosperous careers.

I was taught that if I was breathing, I was supposed to be contributing, giving, sharing, and striving for more. But at this point in my journey, this typically optimistic, faith-filled, African American woman, who fully believed that you could have everything you want if you just try hard enough, felt the unbearable weight of life's glass ceiling on my head.

I felt stuck as a woman who was trying to be heard in a world that seemed to prefer listening to men. Stuck in systems and structures that I loved but that didn't seem to value women and brown women in particular. Stuck in a world where it seemed too easy to sideline bold, brilliant minds that came in full-figured packages. Stuck in my self-imposed ideas of what it meant to be a professional career woman while living another life as a creative. Stuck as I struggled to keep it all separate–while my gifts went unused.

MY GIFTS, MY SUPERPOWERS

Your gifts are those things that make you special, enrich your life, give you joy and make you stand out. Everyone has them. One of my mentors says, "God didn't have time to make a nobody." I've held on to that on the brightest as well as darkest of days.

Your gifts are those precious pieces of you that nearly bring you pain if you're not exercising them. Your gifts superpower you to truly be your best. Your gifts awaken your passions and can keep you up at night.

It's been said: Your gifts are the things that you would do for free because they bring you so much joy.

What would I do for free? What's my gift? It's my voice. My ability to communicate. My skill in using language whether I'm singing, writing, teaching, facilitating, or just telling a story. My gift to the world is my ability to communicate the sentiment of my heart in an impassioned way and as a result, connect to the hearts of others.

Not fully maximizing who I am, not being seen and not operating according to my divine design made me feel like a dead woman walking, just going through the motions.

While in this state of mind, I was asked by a group of career-minded creatives to join a singing group. I felt embarrassed and horrified at the suggestion. Introduce my business associates to my creative self? No way! My thought was, I'm already a woman, I'm already a brown woman, and I have the nerve to be full-figured. How in the world can I be respected as a professional if

I'm "caught" doing something so artistic? As ridiculous as it may sound to you, I felt judged constantly by a world that seemed to have a hard enough time "getting me." I politely eked out something that sounded like, "No, thank you for asking" but on the inside I was thinking, *You have to be insane if you think I'm going to give you something else to judge me with!*

The only problem with my "solution" was that none of what personified me actually changed. I was still gloriously brown, female, full-figured, and gifted to sing.

A CRUSHING LOSS

I was having a great day, fully inhabiting my professional-development-expert self. I felt the energy of my learners soar as I taught them difficult concepts, and they learned, embraced, and retained everything I shared. I felt the energy that comes when you're operating in your own unique excellence. I felt a boldness that made me press into my greatness, stand up straighter, and teach at my highest level of confidence.

And then the phone rang.

I had just given the group an assignment, so I hid away in a private area to take the call. "What? He WHAT?" I gasped, with the weight of the entire world piled on each word. In just a few moments my "runner's high" came crashing to a halt. I had just learned that my grandfather had passed.

There was no replacement. No sub. No friend who could take over. In that moment, instead of feeling my feelings and expressing my grief, I shape-shifted into some robotic amalgamation of myself and taught for hours. It's hard for me to comprehend exactly how I made it through the day even now, so many years later.

All I can convey about the moment is how terrified I felt to express any true and real emotion. I was so concerned that my humanity would be misjudged as unprofessionalism. I was concerned that the space made for my brand of excellence could easily be taken away. I was concerned that the mirage of my success could completely vanish with one misstep. I was concerned that if anyone saw or heard the real me, all the shape-shifting in the world wouldn't protect me from the consequences.

A GIFT IN GETTING OLDER

After this low point in my life, something did change. As the years wore on, I simply started to care less. Sure, there have been some annoyances, but I found a gift in aging. My very unscientific research has borne out this one simple fact time and time again: You care less about the opinions of others as you get older.

I could still read a room, decide whether I wanted to hold court or be a wallflower, follow all the necessary social cues and banter with the best of them; but most importantly, as I got older, I grew my confidence. I grew my gifts.

Over time, I found the boldness to take up more space without apology, instead of just asking life for more. Instead of holding back, I played life more full-out and took more risks. I found spaces and places to use my voice and my gifts, and I found that to be my salvation.

FINDING "THE DIFFERENCE"

Then it happened. I was standing on a platform at a business event. Over a thousand faces were looking up at me, listening to my words. As the facilitator at the event, I was totally committed to sharing the ideas I had studied and uploaded to my memory. I was fully operating in my gift to teach others. Or so I thought.

As I was sharing my teaching points, music started to play in my head. Insistently. I just couldn't get it out. The music in my head was LOUD and getting louder.

This is not as strange as it may sound. Professional facilitators are often in several places at one time mentally. Most of us are transitioning from what we just taught, crafting the language to build a mental runway to our next teaching point or question, staying present in the moment, and connecting with our audiences, all at the same time. So the competing programming in my head was not unusual.

Yes, I was fully in the moment, but I also felt the type of pressure and anxiety that only comes to me when I have to make a risky decision and make it right now.

In addition to connecting with my audience and sharing the teaching points in this business setting, I now had a decision to make. *Do I sing and share this melody in this professional setting to enhance the message I'm teaching? Will that be weird? Are they going to judge me? Will this be considered unprofessional?*

Younger me would have been too afraid to even consider it.

Older me? Now that's another matter entirely.

I did the emotional and professional cost-benefit analysis in a split second and decided...*forget it...what's the worst thing that could happen?*

It felt like falling off a cliff. My voice soared as I cranked out the melody. A little shaky at first. Then I found my footing and let it rip. As I sang, the audience rose to their feet and it was a *moment*. Suddenly, smartphones were in the air recording what was happening as the learners seemed to care less whether they were at a concert, a class, or a conference. As my "selves" came together that day, my audience connected deeply with my teaching. I had delivered my message, reaching my audience on a level I'd never been able to touch before.

Something happened at that moment for me too. Still in a daze as I walked down the stairs off the platform, I was so clear. A boldness and a confidence grew in me from that very instant. I would never forget it. And in that moment, I could care less whether or not a cynic saw a woman, a brown woman, or a full-figured brown woman; what I knew for sure is I had invited my whole self to the party and it felt so good.

Within hours I had flown back to my hometown and before I knew it, I was on another stage. This time I was singing at my church, a megachurch that seats over eight thousand. I was called on to lead a song with our massive choir and found that while I had butterflies, which is my normal, they seemed to be flying in greater alignment than usual. With a sense of calm, I grabbed the microphone.

While I was singing, it occurred to me that the message of the song and the message of the teaching I had given just a day before had similar themes. In a gospel song, the end of the song is referred to as the vamp. The vamp is a part of the song that is unscripted. It's up to the song leader to give this part of the song meaning, emphasis, and life. The song leader literally creates his or her own lyrics at this point and must decide how to give energy and impact to the overall message of the song.

Standing there, leading and shaping the song, I started to recall things I had told my audience of learners the day before, as a teacher. As the ideas started to flood my mind, I sang them out to the congregation. The response was overwhelming as our faith soared and our spirits connected and were encouraged.

I passed the microphone back to the sound engineer and went to my seat quietly knowing I will never forget.

I may be counted out by others who refuse to celebrate my difference, but the most important cheerleader and advocate for me must be me. Bringing my musical self to the teaching arena made me a better teacher; bringing my teaching insight to a musical platform made me a better singer. The more I contemplated it, the more I realized that there were those in my professional and artistic circles who had truly never met me because I unconsciously decided to become a hidden figure in my own life.

Maybe you've heard the expression, "Why fit in when you were born to stand out?"

I made a decision in the moment that my two selves completely merged: Living a life that would put me on a secret menu was not a life for me. Instead, I would bring out, be out, and live out loud **boldly.**

In so many ways I found the difference between who I was and who I could become was within me all along. As a mentor said to me years ago, "You are the problem, and you are the solution." Realizing that fact, and becoming more of who I was destined to be, was the mental switch that minimized the outer negativity –and more importantly–my negativity within.

Alisa Sample-Alexander is a motivational speaker, recording artist, master facilitator, and learning professional. She has co-authored the textbook *Women in Sociology*, as well as *My Unchanging Shepherd*, with her mother, Rubie Sample.

How Breaking Culture Freed My Soul

Dr. Lynne Maureen Hurdle

Two life forces coalesced around the same time in Lynne Maureen Hurdle's life: Having accepted her infertility, Lynne and her husband were preparing to adopt a son; and Lynne's mom died before she could meet her grandson. As Lynne came to terms with the reality that her mom would never have the chance to be the doting grandmother Lynne had wanted her to be. Lynne was now free to "break culture" and parent differently.

In the spring of 1993, I was diagnosed with infertility. My fallopian tubes were damaged and needed to be repaired. This diagnosis was devastating. It was unexpected, unfair, unimaginable and a few more *uns* that I have a feeling you can relate to.

THERE'S GOTTA BE A WAY

Four years into my marriage, I was not ready for this news, but I sprang into action anyway. That was my modus operandi back then: get hit, take it, don't process it; instead, spring into action and find another way.

As a conflict resolution specialist, shifting into problem-solving mode was natural for me even when emotions tried to get in the way. I knew how to take care of emotions. I'd grown up with parents who didn't do emotions well. My mom expressed anger explosively and love confusingly, while my dad literally ran from any emotional expression that opposed my mother's. So, I learned how to shove emotions way back in the corner of my heart, on reflex.

In this situation, my "another way" was to immediately schedule surgery to repair my tubes. When that was unsuccessful, leaving me scarred physically and emotionally, I quickly moved forward with a new plan to try the latest in fertility treatments that might help our dream of parenthood materialize. After all, it was not like there was no hope; so many advances were being made, surely, I could be helped. But when January 1994 rolled in, I was served with the crushing news that this baby thing was not going to happen.

Right away my husband and I decided to start the process of forming a family through adoption. Despite a few raised eyebrows and some loud warnings from well-meaning folk in my African American community, we lovingly went ahead with what I saw as my chance to finally be a mom. Also, the chance to enjoy what so many parents experience: ecstatic grandparents ready and waiting to lovingly "spoil" our child. It was a dream I'd kept for so many years after watching my mom fuss over everyone else's grandchildren, longing desperately to hold her own. My mom was thrilled at the news that we were going to adopt a child, but something was wrong with her.

BLINDED BY THE LIGHT

What was wrong? We didn't know and what was more frightening, the doctors didn't either.

Five years earlier, my mom had suffered in silence through breast cancer. She had shaped us into such an emotionally repressed family that a week after she was diagnosed, she and my dad gathered my sister and me around her spectacularly decorated Christmas tree. Then she announced, "I have breast cancer, now let's open our presents, you know how I love Christmas." We knew that we were not allowed to voice the shock, fear, or the mind-numbing questions screaming within us.

Now with this new crisis, we were supposed to have faith, be brave, and act as if what was happening wasn't the most terrifying thing that our family had ever experienced. We spent the rest of 1994 watching my mom suffer and waste away from what was later diagnosed as the return of her breast cancer. I was not prepared to deal with it.

Faced with the probability that my mom could die, I started to see a side of me that I was not at all familiar with. In the face of real fear, the kind that stops your heart, takes your breath away, and threatens to bring you to your knees, I was barely recognizable to myself. Friends and family, even strangers saw me as this outgoing, funny woman with a giant smile who is always ready for good trouble and a little mischief now and then.

I had met my infertility head on, never allowing it to slow me down, or as the old commercial advised us, I never let them see me sweat. But this crisis with my mom threatened to stop me cold. I was operating in a barely functional depression. I was awake and coherent, putting one foot in front of the other every day, going to work, painfully flashing "that giant smile," crying in the bathroom, and sitting with my mom and my sister at the hospital until visiting hours ended. I would return home, give a report to my husband and other family members, yell at my dad for not dealing with it well, overeat and then throw myself into bed for three to four hours of sleep. Fear and worry were two constant companions that did not let me rest any longer than that.

On the weekends, we were still going full speed ahead with the adoption process. My days were filled with endless paperwork and excruciating hospital visits where we would pretend that everything was going to be alright. I felt like I was carrying a five-hundred-pound weight on my heart causing it to beat so fast that I knew it was close to bursting.

A PASSING, AND AN ARRIVAL

By July, my mom was unexpectedly and unbearably gone. My heart finally allowed itself to break. I was too much in a daze to even think about processing her death. I was operating on autopilot and my only mission was to complete the paperwork for our adoption process. We were so close. I went through the motions–funeral, burial–accepting what felt like a million empty platitudes, and then went back to work. Even though I was a shell of the person I had been, I kept going, laser-focused. I had to make it to motherhood.

A year later, our son came bursting into our lives, and I prayed that the joy would keep me from drowning in the depression. Two weeks in, I was smacked in the face with the reality that my mom was gone and all the parenting questions I had planned on asking were no longer answerable from her voice. She was not here to hold or even know her beautiful grandson. I didn't know any other mothers who were experiencing this. They all had their moms supporting them with their grandmotherly love and wisdom. I felt the loss of my mom as if it had just happened all over again. It hurled me into deeper darkness.

The depression overwhelmed me. Even though I knew that my mom's fierce grandma love would have been accompanied by relentless commentary on my parenting, I still ached for her to fill that role. Every time I called my aunts or a friend, scared out of my mind about what to do about a milestone not reached yet, or the high fevers that our son held onto for days, I would burst into tears afterwards as I wondered what my mom's advice would have been.

LOVE DON'T COME EASY

Like a lot of people, my relationship with my mom was complicated. In our house, she was the one in charge and everyone knew it. Interestingly enough, my relationship with my dad did not become complicated until my mom got sick, but that's a story for another book. My mom was 5 foot 3, yet her presence was commanding. Her method of parenting was to mix love with total control.

When my sister Gayle and I were little, she stayed home, loved on us, took us everywhere, and even sewed almost everything we wore. Gayle and I are thirteen months apart so pushing us toward the same interests came easy for my mom. She enrolled us in a variety of classes but rarely took notice of how we felt about them. Gayle hated dance, and I was terrible at sewing. We both went into our teen years doing things that our mom wanted us to do, having learned at an early age that speaking up to her would cost us dearly. We'd get yelled at or be subjected to the silent treatment, or become the topic of her marathon telephone conversations with her friends. Social media could never compete with the network of girlfriends my mom shared life's ups and downs with.

She was both a champion warrior and worrier. I watched her fight for us against racist principals, other kids' parents, teachers, and any adults who dared to cross her or harm us. As a warrior, she was never afraid to speak up and show us that she loved us. As a worrier, she gained tighter control by joining every school and church committee that oversaw anything that we were involved in.

Rather than manage her fears, she drove us to almost every social activity and chaperoned us once we got there. She unabashedly commented on our every thought, decision, friend, and love interest, leaving no space for me to be my own person and find my own voice.

But she was my mom, and she was gone forever. I spent my entire first year of motherhood crying every day. One day after being shamed by some family members for lugging a baby carrier to a family event, when I "should have known" that it was unnecessary because everyone would just hold him, I gave up. I no longer wanted to rack my brain thinking about who to call each time I needed the comfort of an experienced mother's wisdom. I was a motherless mother and I had to come to grips with that and everything that it meant.

FREE TO BREAK CULTURE

I had a terrifying and liberating thought: As a new mother, parenting without her mother, I had the freedom to make up my own parenting rules. I decided to harness the power of that kind of freedom and run with it. I am not celebrating the fact that my mother dying presented me with this new way to live; rather, I am honoring it as a pivotal event in my life.

With my mom no longer around, I had the opportunity to **break culture.** Being raised by Black parents from the south was a pretty common denominator in my circle of friends and family when I was growing up. As a result, parenting strategies were somewhat universal. As a teen, I remember a group of us sitting around telling all the same stories of spankings, punishment, long-winded lectures, and classic one-liners meant to put you in your place.

Don't get me wrong, this was not just a complaining circle. There was plenty of laughter, but certainly no rebellious talk of breaking away from any of it when we became parents. In fact, we knew we were going to carry on those same behaviors with our own children and we couldn't wait. But all that happened long before I chose the study and work of conflict resolution.

By the time I became a mom, I had over ten years of taking and leading workshops on communication, mediation, negotiation, and hosting difficult conversations. I had accumulated a wealth of experience teaching the strategies and techniques that worked so well in conflict situations to educators and leaders, many of whom were parents.

The problem was none of this was popular in my African American family or among the people who shared my upbringing. In fact, it could be and would be cause for ridicule, eye-rolling, and being outrightly dismissed as going against the culture. By deciding to do this my way, I was making a very conscious choice to **break culture** and bring in all of the knowledge I had gathered and was continuing to absorb in my conflict resolution work. It was a big leap, but my husband, a southern man himself, said he was all on board. I jumped right in and began to look at conflict in a deeper way. I started with looking at discipline and what I had been taught about it. Then I extended my efforts by examining the relationship I had with conflict.

HOMEMADE SOUL FOOD

It was a good thing, too, because six years later when our next son came into our family, my life really changed. Conflict became a regular occurrence. It's not that our oldest son did not provide plenty of opportunities to confront conflict; it's just that he was less in love with it, and we saw more things eye to eye.

As soon our second son could talk, he questioned and pushed back against just about everything and everyone. The worst part was, even in his most contrary moments, he managed to be incredibly likable and enjoyable. On top of all of this, my husband, who had said that he was down for this new style of parenting, did his best to avoid conflict. Either that, or he exploded during conflict. I had a real team to learn from.

The work I was doing on myself was paying off in big ways. I was enjoying being a mom. I learned how to navigate the gaping hole in my heart by grieving and feeling the absence of one of the most important people in my life. I was sitting down and talking to my sons when they were uncooperative or cranky. If I slipped up and started yelling a lot, I searched myself for what I was feeling and why, then shared those revelations with them along with an apology. I hosted family meetings regularly where we would talk about the conflicts that were happening.

Everyone had a voice. I was using a lot of conflict resolution techniques when my husband and I disagreed. It wasn't easy. There was plenty of pushback. My sons weren't always in the mood to talk it out and there was often eye-rolling at my suggestions of family meetings in the beginning.

There was also the time when my husband had just finished venting about something that I had done that really ticked him off. I paraphrased back his complaints perfectly, to let him know that I had heard him (just like I taught in my workshops). Then he looked me straight in the eyes and said, "Do not use that conflict resolution crap on me!" That story makes me laugh to this day.

Using the skills in my personal life meant I was walking the talk and I was proud. I was getting to know myself and using my voice to stand up for this new way of parenting.

The results I was getting led me to think about my clients and a question that I had been sitting with for years. My workshops were always packed, and folks not only enjoyed them, but they often told me how important and useful they thought the skills were. The question was, *why weren't they using them in their lives?* I knew for a fact that they weren't practicing the skills.

The lessons I was learning in my personal life needed to be applied to my work. What if I could go beyond just teaching the skills? What if I could also share the difficulties, rewards, and mechanics of using them by sharing my own experiences? I believed that my clients would then start to apply the skills in their lives. I changed up my whole teaching game. I became vulnerable, revealing what I learned about myself in conflicts so they could see themselves in me and be inspired to at least try to use what they were learning.

THE SOUL OF CONFLICT

I began to work in a different, more personal way with my clients. I helped them explore "The Soul of Conflict" – the place where old conflict wounds reside. I taught them to identify and acknowledge the effect of these wounds on them. I showed them how to sit in and work through their feelings and then release them. I watched the work transform them. The more *I* lived it, the better *their* results. My business was taking off in ways it never had before. I have continued to thrive in the work.

I would have never chosen for it to happen this way. I love my mom and miss her every day, but the truth is that in the midst of the most heartbreaking situation of my life, I found myself, my voice, and a way of working that changes lives.

Dr. Lynne Maureen Hurdle is a communication expert and conflict resolution strategist; a diversity, equity, and inclusion facilitator; and a writer. She blends the connection between communication, conflict and culture into her unique style of engagement for leaders.

How Boxing Uncaged Me

Malissa Smith

Malissa Smith had been fascinated with boxing ever since she was a young girl. When she finally stepped into a boxing gym as a woman in her 40s, it set her free in ways she could not have imagined –and it began her journey toward becoming one of the world's foremost authorities on women's boxing.

Crossing the threshold of the storied boxing mecca, Gleason's Gym in Brooklyn's DUMBO neighborhood, I always feel as if I have entered an altered dimension of space and time.

I am at once in my element. The thudding echoes of fists connecting on the heavy-bag. The rapid *da-da-da-da-da-da* of the speed bag. The ring-clock bell intoning the signal to end another three-minute round. The alighted "Hey champ," of my latest trainer, Lennox Blackmoore. All of it locates me. Feasts my eyes and ears with sights and sounds I love. And breathing in. Absorbing warmth and dimensions of sweaty days and nights of boxing, I am one with it. I smile too. No matter my mood. My attitude. My feelings. Whether tired or sad or aggrieved or stressed. Whether I feel surrounded by love or alone in my own morass of darkness.

My usual routine is sixteen three-minute rounds of training with a sixty-second interval between each round. I shadow box for four rounds. Going through my boxing sequences of left jabs and straight rights, hooks and uppercuts, body punches and overhand rights, alone as a solo dancer in the ring and sometimes in concert with others. We each find our own spaces. Respect the outpouring of skills and sweat. Smile and nod our greetings as we chart our paths through the ring.

Once warmed up, I work on the pads for four rounds with Lennox. Holding up two paddles, he calls out shots for me to throw. Or I know how to execute just by the positioning of the paddles. Sometimes the shots are fluid, my feet in concert with my hands, deft and light and easy. On my off days, I can expect a shot to the head and a "Wake up girl!" admonition.

After pads, I hit the double-end bag. A rounded ball, it is tethered to a crossbeam above and held down on the ground by a hook chained to a fifty-pound weight.

On my best days, I feel weightless, as if enclosed in a zero-gravity chamber. I bounce from side to side, in a flow of varying shot selections and movement. I lose myself. Feel the oneness of my body movements as they strike the moving bag. I flick the sweat. Inhalations and exhaled grunts punctuating my punches.

I end my boxing day with four rounds on the speed bag. I have become highly proficient. I execute sequenced back-and-forth rhythms of punches before doubling up for thirty-second spurts. I also dance around it. Taking rounds of up jabs and quick rights. Emulating punches to the head. Working on quickness and pivots; executing actions at odd angles.

It is my beginning. My ring of power. My moments of self within self when it's just me and my show of strength. My ever-changing range of being as I step into my jab to propel myself sometimes forward, sometimes back, sometimes side to side.

MY LOVE AFFAIR WITH BOXING IS A LONG ONE

On my tough Manhattan block in the early 1960s, 12th Street between First and Second Avenues, even at the age of nine, I could discern the science. Knew that when it came to boys fighting on the sidewalk, the ones who threw wild, swinging punches were unschooled. The calmer ones, the boys who knew the game, held their arms close to their bodies, releasing jabs and straight rights with an effortless quickness before artfully slipping left or right from an opponent's telegraphed punches. They displayed that uncanny boxer's instinct for offense and defense before walking away, largely unscathed, while the other boys crowded around their fallen comrade.

And there I was, sometimes the lone girl at such showings, back behind the crowd, on the periphery, but always admiring. I was a comic book kid then, too. I read *Superman*, *Superboy*, and *Supergirl*. They were always in fights, those three, but their purposes were never personal. They were always fighting for something. For justice. For the rights of the bullied. For light. It's why I couldn't read *Batman* then. Too dark. His anger seething out from his bat cave at night. What I craved was lightness. Effortlessness. The science of it. The freedom.

When I was twelve, my Uncle Mel taught me the proper way to throw a jab followed by a straight right. I never felt prouder than when I executed the combination correctly. I'd step into the jab, throwing my hand from its perch at the left side of my face and extending it out, twisting it so that the third knuckle of my left hand aligned perfectly straight with my shoulder. Keeping my right hand at the right side of my head, I'd follow up the jab by extending my right hand with the same twisting motion, while also turning my hip and the right ball of my foot. This gave me momentum and power.

I practiced that one-two across my lifetime. Wanting more than anything to box, but never quite making the leap to knowing that I, as a girl, could walk into a boxing gym at any time to learn the science of the ring.

What I could and did do was watch boxing. My boxing heroes were heavyweights, like Muhammad Ali, and Kenny Norton with an overhand right that felt like devastation, even observing it through the flickering lights of a television set. Later, I grew to love watching middleweights, like Sugar Ray Leonard and Marvelous Marvin Hagler and Roberto Duran.

JOURNEYING TO THE RIGHT LIFE

I woke up one day at the age of thirty-seven and realized I was living the wrong life. That was in 1991. I was talking with my therapist, Elaine, about boxing then too. It was my invisible guideline back to my girlhood self.

Elaine had told me she'd just joined a boxercise program at Gold's Gym on the Upper West Side of Manhattan. I thought, "That's for me!" but in an uncharacteristic fit of impetuosity decided to chuck it all and go out into the world instead. Within a month I had given up my apartment and put my stuff in storage, distressing my friends. But I went anyway despite their protestations and fear. After a round of quick goodbyes, I made my way to Greece for the summer, and pressed on to Israel and the Sinai desert in the early fall.

If I'd woken up to a sense of being on the wrong path, being in the world meant I could face the fact that I had lost myself. The thread of my being seemingly gone, I saw myself as bifurcated: a physical being and a formless mind. Invisible.

The break came one afternoon. I was in the small toilet room at the Al-Arab Youth Hostel in the Arab Quarter of the Old City in Jerusalem. I watched myself from above and below as if I were a balloon. Struggling mightily, I managed to integrate myself, only to experience the splitting again in an outdoor café later that evening. This time I was up above in a tree, feeling the night breezes as so many tender kisses on my forehead.

Back in New York, Elaine proclaimed that my breakdown had started to integrate me. I couldn't see it. Yet her tenderness was affecting. Provided me with a touchstone as I contended with my sense of loss. This was when I wrote my list. It had four things: Write, travel, join the Peace Corps, and box.

Traveling again, but this time with a little more thought, I made my way across Asia for five months as I waited to receive my Peace Corps posting.

I felt myself opening. Writing my experiences in journals picked up along the way. Reveling in the small moments. Hearing and listening and eventually spending ten days of silent meditation in a Buddhist Temple. Gaining a sense of camaraderie with the travelers I met. Boxing still pulling me as I became aware of the martial aspects that underlay many of the countries I visited.

In Japan, I seemed to walk among the ghosts of Samurai; in Thailand, I watched Thai boxing matches in far-flung places. On temple grounds, vacant lots, and open fields, kids, men––but no women that I saw––would contest in the heat of the evening under bright lights. With night market cart owners hawking food next to women selling pineapples cleverly spun around long sticks.

China proved to be another haven for martial practices. I was surprised by the ubiquity of Tai Chi in the early morning, in cities and small towns across the breadth of China. In one end-of-the-world place in Inner Mongolia, blue Mao-suited practitioners would take over the streets at 6:00 a.m., urged on by the strains of martial music blaring through loudspeakers high up on lampposts.

The beauty and symmetry of the practice enthralled me, but it was boxing I craved. I was thrilled by the glimpses I caught on a shared television near my hotel. People perched on tiny stools clustered around the screen, somehow avoiding the long series of extension cords snaking back through a window. Nosing my way in, I felt a bit in heaven watching a boxing match in progress, the two fighters skillfully slugging away. The ten or so onlookers were animated as they yelled out instructions, as if the fighters could hear them. At once a part of the collective, I, too, bobbed and weaved with tiny movements as the images shimmered in front of us.

It would take me another four years to finally make my way to the sport. Asia had come and gone, plus a two-year stint living in the Russian Far East as a Peace Corps volunteer. At last back in the United States, living in Brooklyn, I had faced another sort of challenge: a large tumor growing through my brachial plexus. The growth was lying beside my lung and only accessible through the "Broadway" of the muscles, veins, and artery in my neck.

Having come through the eight and half hours of surgery with a benign clearance, followed by ten weeks of physical therapy to regain the use of my right arm, I figured it was high time I gave boxing a try. After all, I'd faced down an emotional breakdown, and the divide that is life and death, or so it seemed. What was boxing compared to that?

CROSSING THE DIVIDE

My first foray into boxing was at Eastern Athletics. A rather upscale gym in Brooklyn Heights, it occupied the basement of the old St. George Hotel, a once-glamorous destination for weddings and anniversary parties through the early 1960s. On Thursdays, as Halloween made its way toward Thanksgiving, I'd lightly jog from my apartment to a small ring that had been set up, along with a speed bag and a heavy bag. The class had about ten people and as surly an instructor as I had ever met. To say it was a failure was an understatement. I had no idea of what his unintelligibly barked commands meant, but one thing was clear: What I had thought was a perfect one-two combination was nothing of the kind, and only made him grumpier.

I was grateful when the four-week mini class ended. I did not sign up for the next one, opting instead to nurse my pride and find the courage to seek out Gleason's Gym.

"No more excuses," I said aloud to myself, on a crisp clear day in early January as I made the sojourn to DUMBO.

With low wintry light streaming in through the line of grimy windows facing the street, I was immediately greeted by the owner of the gym, Bruce Silverglade, seated at a desk near the entrance. A chessboard in mid-game took up a corner of the desk.

"Hi, can I help you?" Bruce asked.

I introduced myself and within seconds he was up and out of his seat and touring me through the cavernous expanse. As the sights and sounds hit my senses, calm descended. I had found my place.

By the end of my tour, I had paid a month's dues–thirty dollars a month in those days–and arranged my first training session at 7:30 the following morning, with an old-school trainer named Johnny Grinage.

As trainers went, Johnny was as classic as they came: gruff, salty, heart of gold, a lot of self-aggrandizement, and talkative.

We quickly found a shared love of 1950s jazz which meant that he would not only lecture me on all things boxing, but also regale me with a series of stories on repeat about players like Wynton Kelly and Miles Davis, both of whom had boxed over the years.

Those first forays with Johnny saw me learning and relearning on an endless loop beginning with warm-up calisthenics using a broomstick, four rounds of jumping rope, and light shadow boxing in front of the mirror. I did this three mornings a week.

During the first month Johnny had me throw punches at a side bag attached to the wall.

The rhythm became a dance: *jab, jab, straight right, left hook, bob and weave, straight right, left hook, straight right, bob and weave, repeat.*

After eight rounds, he'd have me do the same thing moving back and forth along a slip rope: a clothesline strung between two poles at about shoulder height to mimic the likely trajectory of a shot to my jaw.

With each punch came a string of admonitions.

"I don't want no pitty-pat. Now you *hit*, or don't bother."

Then he'd shout, "Not like that, like this," though I was never quite certain what he meant, because by the time I turned, his demonstration was over.

When I got it right, Johnny would say, "Now *that's* what I'm talking about, no pitty-pat."

FINDING MY POWER

The day I graduated to the heavy bag felt like a celebration, as did the new more elaborate ritual of wrapping my hands, enfolding extra foam padding to protect my knuckles, because, I came to learn, "no pitty-pat" meant damaging my hands through the soft padding of my old, borrowed gloves.

As I learned to hit hard though, the tears came; water leaking from my eyes as a release of some deep-seated pain with every punch I threw.

Tears bit through the combinations I'd throw, sometimes twelve punches in a row. My power slammed against the unforgiving stoniness of the heavy bag, fists willing it to sway.

I'd move around the bag, catching it with yet more punches in combination. Johnny's voice in my ear shouting, "Now hit it like you *mean* it."

My arms tired as the rounds grew from four to eight to twelve in an unrelenting blur of punches.

I'd hit and hit and hit. Tears and sweat mingled, blurring my vision at times. I'd swipe them away between punches. Hit the bag again.

I was in a beatdown. Each dig to the body, each hook to the head, a blow that pummeled me to release each pain in my soul. Ripping at the scar tissue in a merciless battle.

If I'd felt my body bifurcate in Jerusalem, my unrelenting war with the heavy bag tore away at my mind. It stripped me bare into the very sinews of my fears, brimming with all the things I hadn't been able to face. Crushing emotions long hidden behind the layers of well-defended fortifications I had encased myself in.

Johnny yelling, "I don't want to see no pitty-pat," became a mantra for everything I did. Learning to attack things as I saw them. Pushing myself as twelve rounds became sixteen and on to twenty.

I AM A BOXING WARRIOR

After a while, Johnny would have me come in on Saturday mornings to spar. My body in the armor of a boxing warrior. Gloved, helmeted, and wearing a groin protector, covered with a patina of palpable fear as I screamed inside, *How can I really hit someone?*

I didn't mind getting hit; the punches weren't that hard. And I was learning defense. Learning the control. Learning slipping, and bobbing and weaving, and raising my arms to fend jabs and hooks and body blows. It was hitting that was hard. Punching someone else with force. Seeking out vulnerabilities. Feeling triumphant in landing a double jab on an opponent's face. Or a shot to the gut that pushed my opponent back a bit.

Tears came again. Behind my headgear. Giant stings as I'd reach out to pound. My emotions a jumble of unintelligible grunts and heavy breaths. Hidden from view but exposed in my own mind.

I am a fraud for thinking I can box.

Who am I kidding? I am cheating again.

Then the claustrophobia would attack me as I'd paw away to get my gloves off. Racked by panic, by the discomfort of my mouthguard making me retch, by the borrowed leather helmet caked with years of sweat, by my own giant puffball hands, my mind screaming *failure*. I wasn't worthy of wearing any of it.

Back on the bag, I'd pummel it again.

And it all became so familiar.

The ritual of morning. Walking to the gym in any weather. Grinning with a little extra jaunt to my step, each entry a new beginning. Each round a metaphor for what life is.

Then the warmups. Getting my hands wrapped. Listening to Johnny's story about the time his wife sang with Wynton Kelly's trio, or the one about how Miles Davis used to train at Gleason's when it was on 30th Street in Manhattan. And hitting the bag. Each round feeling like a small existence: like a walking meditation with a beginning and an ending and a period of renewal before beginning again.

Gradually getting faster and more precise. Learning my skills. Getting less and less weary. Finding the rhythm in hitting the bag. Hard. Sensing where the bag would give even when it felt as if I was hitting a brick wall.

Sitting on the apron of a ring and feeling a sense of peace. Fist-bumping my morning crew pals. The trainers and the boxers, like me, at the gym to work it all out on the bag, whatever that meant and wherever it would take them. Those were my mornings. The feeling of my circle growing around me with each extension of my jab, in any direction I moved.

My boxing journey began long ago on 12th Street, but it continues in each stride I make in and out of the ring.

If there is one thing boxing taught me, it is that fear and the accompanying self-doubt has been, and continues to be, my nemesis. It lives with me as a shadow being that I face down every time I glove up. I know it from the tears. The ones that still well up when I haven't given myself the self-care I deserve. I know it from the places where new scar tissue has formed from hurts that have gone unanswered.

Whether it's hitting a bag or responding to one's lived experience, it's the commitment to the task that matters. And, as Johnny would say, "No pitty-pat allowed."

Malissa Smith is a writer and the author of A *History of Women's Boxing,* the first definitive history of the sport. She is a global female boxing authority and co-host of the "WAAR Room" sports podcast.

The Courage to Change Your Choices

Caroline de Posada

Motivational speaker and life coach Caroline de Posada lived her life in the in-between: Her immigrant family's expectation that she pursue success as a lawyer, and the heartstrings that pulled her toward the same path as her famous, unconventional father. Through her journey, Caroline learned the power of summoning the courage to break from the identities and labels imposed on her to live a healthier, happier and more meaningful life.

"What are you going to do once the baby is born?" my colleague asked as we waited for the judge to take the bench. I was due to give birth that day but with no signs of labor coming on, I had decided to declare myself "ready for trial."

I put my hand on my oversized belly and shrugged my shoulders. "I'll find a nanny during maternity leave and then come back to work."

Wasn't that what all working women did?

It had all seemed so simple—until I held my firstborn son in my arms.

With paid maternity leave, I didn't need to worry about logistics at first, but as the time neared for me to go back to my regular schedule, I realized I was no longer the same woman who had announced herself "ready for trial" on her due date.

WHAT GOT YOU HERE WON'T
NECESSARILY GET YOU THERE

I don't remember a time when I hadn't planned to be a lawyer. "You've been saying you want to be a lawyer since you were 5 years old!" my mom would say.

In my immigrant family, our generation's definition of success boiled down to becoming a lawyer or a doctor. My grandfather had been a lawyer in Cuba. And at 47 years old, he had become a lawyer in the United States. As an immigrant who had gone to law school for a second time and passed the bar in a new language, he was the pride of our family.

"You're just like your grandfather," they'd tell me.

I adopted that identity with pride.

But I had a wild card in my life: my father, Joachim de Posada.

Although he'd studied to be a psychologist, he'd built a career as a motivational speaker. My father was untraditional in every sense of the word—family, career, you name it.

He was also my favorite person.

With my dad, I entered a different world full of incredible people, ideas, and energy. This lover of life often suggested that I could be a speaker, too. Then we could travel the world together!

But that wasn't a viable career choice for me. I wanted to get married and raise children, not be divorced and on the road all the time like him.

During my last year of university, a conversation with my dad sparked the possibility of my traveling with him and managing his colorful career. At 21 years old, I was about to graduate, and this was my chance to experience my dad's life before settling down. Why not? I didn't even have a boyfriend!

The idea was exciting, but my family had concerns. "If you do this now, you'll never go to law school," my mother warned. "All I ever wanted was to see my granddaughter follow in my footsteps," my grandfather lamented.

I knew what I was *supposed* to do, but my heart wanted this time with my father more than anything. I made a promise to my mother and grandfather and swore to honor it. "Two years," I pledged, "and then I'll go to law school."

And after two years on the road, I kept that promise. I am grateful I did because it was during my years in law school that I met my future husband and created the life I thought would have been impossible if I had followed in my dad's footsteps.

WHEN THE PATH YOU CHOSE NO LONGER SERVES YOU

I had loved being an attorney at the Public Defender's office but now I wanted to stay at home with my son. The desire to be a professional with a thriving career washed away from me.

My husband and I couldn't easily afford to have me stop working. Losing an income would present consequences, but I quit anyway.

And it wasn't long before the novelty of being home all the time wore off. Just like that yearning to stay home with my child had crept up on me, so did my longing to work again. Though this longing for work looked different. I wanted extra income and a challenge outside housework and child-rearing, but I wanted to be a mom more than a career woman.

Random life circumstances (and a bachelor's degree in accounting) led me to start a small bookkeeping business that served my lawyer friends. This offered an easy way to supplement our family income and work from home during my son's naps.

I liked this work. It wasn't as all-consuming as practicing law, and I found it fun and challenging.

My decisions invited plenty of opinions.

Friends and family questioned—with more judgment than curiosity—why I had bothered to go to law school. Had I taken out all those student loans for nothing?

"Why bother spending hundreds of thousands of dollars on a degree you're not going to use?" asked one dear relative.

"You studied for seven years and spent all that money to be a bookkeeper?" scoffed a friend.

Their comments made me question my choices even though those choices offered me the freedom to live life on my own terms and gave me the ability to explore motherhood without conflict.

Isn't it incredible that we can feel happy and fulfilled and still think we're doing something wrong because others don't agree with us?

As my friend and hypnotherapist Adrianna Foster says: "Too often we build a life that confines us or molds into people's expectations. And we defend that life—even if we have to go against ourselves to keep it. Because deep down inside we believe that the life we truly want will not be accepted or well received. Rather than be rejected, we silence our soul."

As the years passed, one son became three sons. I eased my way back into the legal profession and closed the bookkeeping side job. I opened a homeowner's association law practice which allowed me to juggle between honoring my profession and making sure I was at my kids' Easter egg hunts and home with them when they got sick.

During those years, I often fantasized about becoming a speaker and author. I imagined what it would be like to share a stage with my dad and do the work he did. But I carried my laundry list of reasons why it was better to tuck those fantasies back into my dream box.

It's easy to feel locked into a path because we think we're too far along to turn back or head in a different direction.

AWAKENINGS OF THE SOUL

For 35 years I created a narrative about what I could and couldn't do based on my age, gender, and other people's expectations.

The choices I made served me well, but what made my soul truly come alive were those moments when I got to participate in my dad's world—personal development conferences and workshops, mastermind groups, inspiring conversations, and exchanges of ideas. Those doses of inspiration kept me going until the next time I could join him.

I treasured the two years I had spent traveling with my father and managing his career.

Even though I had honored my word to my family and become a lawyer, I took every opportunity I could to be part of my dad's work. I loved when he conducted seminars in Miami that I could sit in on. I even took my boys to watch their grandpa shine on stage.

One evening my husband, Orlando, and I were having a date night, which meant sitting on the couch, sipping some wine and praying that none of our boys would wake up.

We struck up a conversation about my dad. "I love that you two have such a great relationship," my husband said. "How did you manage that when he was never around?"

"Hold that thought," I replied, and tiptoed upstairs to grab a box that had traveled with me to every home I'd ever lived in. It was black, rectangular and deep and once held a gift from my dad.

I placed the box on the coffee table and opened it. Hundreds of postcards and letters spilled out. One by one, we read through them. Some were funny, others were emotional, and some were mundane, but taken together, there on that coffee table my entire relationship with my dad was scribbled onto a lifetime of postcards.

"Now I get it," Orlando said. "You two should write a book about this! You should teach divorced dads how to be there even when they're not."

We grew excited about the idea and soon afterwards, we invited my dad over for dinner. After we ate, I grabbed the box. "Dad, I want to show you something. I am so grateful for all the effort you put in to stay close to me over the years."

Tears streamed down my dad's face as he held in his hands the postcards he had written. He had no idea I had kept them all these years.

Orlando shared his idea with my dad and urged us to consider writing a *Be There Even When You're Not* book together.

At first my dad hesitated. "I am no parenting expert. I just did the best I could to stay connected to my daughter." But as time passed, he became as excited as I was about this project.

For my dad, this became the culmination of his work—the story of him and his daughter. For me, this idea unlocked the dreams I had to one day speak alongside my dad. The plan was always that I would help write the book and make the occasional appearance, but my dad would be the one doing the bulk of the traveling and speaking. This arrangement would allow me to dip my toe in the water without compromising my priorities.

The book project began, until we encountered an X factor neither of us could control.

Cancer.

My larger-than-life dad was originally diagnosed with prostate cancer when I was 17 years old. Maybe the confrontation I had with his mortality is what gave me the courage to put my studies on hold and travel with him for those years.

The treatment was successful and my father continued his life and work for the next ten years until they detected kidney cancer.

He got the news the day I took the Florida Bar exam. The good news was the cancer was detected early. Removing the kidney would solve the problem. Three weeks post-surgery, dad was speaking onstage again.

A few years passed until a routine checkup revealed a more serious problem: bladder cancer. This time things weren't so simple. The doctor explained that bladder cancer was aggressive and understudied. Things could get bad quickly.

Although these confrontations with my dad's health were scary at first, his attitude taught me a lot about how I wanted to live my life. I learned to focus on the present moment rather than worry about the unknown future, approach the good and bad news with a stoic mindset, and practice the art of carrying on.

My father was extremely proactive with his care. He was obedient when it came to treatment, procedures, and doctor's appointments but rebellious about letting cancer change his life.

For as long as he could, my father treated cancer like an accessory to his life. It was something he managed, not something that managed him. I often joked that the doctors had confused my dad's lab work with someone else's because his lifestyle never matched his test results—until things got bad. And just as the doctor had warned me years before, they got really bad, really quickly.

There came a point when my father could no longer stay ahead of the disease. He went from playing tennis five times a week (with cancer all over his body), writing, speaking, and traveling, to becoming too ill for us to focus on anything other than his care.

The unfathomable was happening: My first love was dying.

As I sat by him on his deathbed, I clung to my best friend, mentor, and teacher.

"I don't know how I'm going to live without you, dad. I'm not only losing you; I'm losing the world you've created, too—the conferences and seminars we attend together, the books you recommend, the incredible conversations we have. I have no idea how to find these things without you."

I couldn't bear to say that I was also losing the dream of writing our book together but my dad knew what this all meant and he was at peace with it. He smiled and squeezed my hand. "Don't worry, *mi amor,* that world is going to find you. And about the book … whether you finish it or not doesn't matter. Our story has already been written. You are my greatest accomplishment, my love."

NEW BEGINNINGS

Sometimes we voluntarily choose a new direction, but sometimes life forces us into paths we're not quite ready for.

My life as I knew it had died.

What once felt safe now felt stifling.

Things no longer made sense. I had prided myself on doing things the right way, but right according to whom? The rules we're born into? The rules society imposes on us? The rules we create in our minds?

I had lost the opportunity to realize a dream of sharing the stage with my dad because I'd wasted so much time writing a different 35-year-long narrative.

Despite experiencing sadness and regret, I was energized by the thought that I could still honor my dad's legacy by following in his footsteps and continuing his work.

At first I tried to juggle being a mom, wife, and attorney while becoming an author and speaker on the side—but the time had come for me to own my calling.

THE DIFFERENCE

What had made all the difference in my life *were* the intermittent detours I had taken on my path to becoming a successful lawyer: the choice to travel with my dad in between college and law school, the choice to leave the Public Defender's Office so I could stay home with my son, the choice to work as a bookkeeper as I figured things out. These choices were not deviations from my path; they were awakenings of my soul—tiny acts of courage that were preparing me for something bigger.

Although becoming a lawyer was an important part of my journey, I now understood that I graduated from law school to have the *choice* to practice law—and also the choice *not* to.

I had been in training to do my father's work for my entire life. It was time to break away from the identities and labels I had adopted along the way.

Life is nothing but a series of choices. You do not have to be married to any one path because of a decision made in a previous season. The decisions and choices you make will bring consequences, and those consequences will become part of your new journey. But you should never forget the power of having a choice.

Starting a new career path didn't come without challenges.

I struggled between releasing the little girl who wanted to walk in her father's shoes and stepping into the shoes of the woman I wanted to be.

It was a time of grieving, stumbling, keeping my head up, and becoming.

But the Universe guided me toward the path I was meant to take—so much so that a spontaneous vacation turned into a near-death experience. After my family and I found ourselves stranded at the edge of a cliff, I was prompted to write my first book: *Looking Over the Edge: A True Story of Facing Fear, Finding Your Way, and All the Lessons In Between.*

I learned to keep my eyes open to the magic, look for the lessons, and keep showing up.

Today I work as a life coach who helps people with mindset, wellness, and relationships. I developed a methodology for bridging the gap between where you are and where you want to be called CORE (Clarity, Organization, Resilience, and Emotional Intelligence) and I used that methodology to pave my path in this work.

Although I write and speak as my father did, my business looks nothing like his—except for our mutual mission to inspire people to lead happier, healthier, and more meaningful lives, and to define success on their own terms.

We often get stuck on who we "are" rather than focusing on the choices we get to make.

Throughout your life you may live in many houses, and you may become many different things. Rather than view identities and labels as boxes that define and contain you, see each of them as one of the many buildings you'll inhabit, decorate to suit your tastes, and either stay in or move on from.

No one can take the skills, experience, and knowledge you'll acquire away from you—and *you* get to define how you'll apply them to realize your next creation.

For a long time I thought I had lost the opportunity to share a stage with my father because I had waited too long to become a speaker. But I've spent the last five years sharing the stage with my father—in my heart, mind, and literally, through video!

My dad was right. His world did find me, and it is a privilege to be a part of it.

There is no one path you have to be locked into.

Choose the next right thing for you—regardless of what others may tell you and despite any doubts about whether or not you're *supposed* to.

You are not locked into a path just because you started down it. You have the choice to change your choices.

Caroline de Posada is an international bilingual speaker, author, and life coach. In her current work, she blends personal development with her gift of storytelling to inspire action in those she serves.

Reflections on Courage

Courage is not stubbornness; it isn't an act of rashness, nor is it a personal value that we like to abide by, such as respect for others or kindness. Courage requires a willingness to go deep within, to listen to our ideas and inclinations, even when they may surprise us or feel inconvenient. It requires us to seize our desire to move forward in life BECAUSE we have listened to the inner voice.

"The word *courage* comes from the same stem as the French word *coeur*, meaning 'heart,'" psychologist Rollo May, author of the classic *The Courage to Create*, reminds us. "Thus just as one's heart, by pumping blood to one's arms, legs, and brain enables all the other physical organs to function, so courage makes possible all the psychological virtues. Without courage other values wither away into mere facsimiles of virtue."

The authors in *The Difference* show us the entire palette of courage that may be required of us if we wish to move into our new age. They tell of moral courage, of physical courage, of social courage. And, as Rollo May points out, the courage to create.

FIND THE COURAGE TO BREAK CULTURE

Dr. Lynne Maureen Hurdle describes how she had to be willing to break some norms if she were to listen to her inner voices. Lynne calls this process of norms-busting "breaking culture," and she exhorts us to scrupulously examine which parts of our culture(s) we may need to relinquish.

"I define 'breaking culture' as a decision to step away from some of the cultural norms and habits that are passed down from generation to generation," Lynne explains. "I'm talking about the venerable 'rules of the game' that pretty much everyone in the culture knows and lives, laughs, and loves by. You have to decide which culture has the strongest influence on you and the way you live your life."

"You don't break culture by accident, in my defining of it. Breaking culture isn't easy," Lynne reminds us. "Along the way, I found many obstacles—including myself. You might be unpopular for a while and face negative comments from those who share that particular culture, but you can choose to stand your ground and keep changing. When you catch yourself being informed by old ways, forgive yourself, decide how you want to change course, and then do it and stick to it."

Lynne has learned that we are often our own biggest obstacle. Observe yourself.

LEARN TO QUIET YOUR FEARS

Listening to our inner voice may, at times, feel more like having a conversation with the devil. Alisa Sample-Alexander knows.

"I am convinced that the most critical voice I've ever heard and actually listened to is my own inner critic," Alisa explains. "It's the enemy on the inside that can often be the most lethal to your personal and professional life. I found it complicated, frustrating, and disempowering to attempt to live my life out playing the 'appropriate' role for the occasion. The person I was presenting as was a facet of my persona, but not my authentic self. Read the room of course but it's highly likely that there's a version of you that you have yet to fully reveal."

There is no shortcut around facing our fears. Alisa describes the mind hacks that helped her find the courage to reveal a more authentic version of herself: "I decided that the time to quiet my fears and bring more of the real me to the table was now. The new guiding thought for my future came from a scripture I love that I believe holds value whether you're a particularly spiritual person or not. Matthew 5:14-15 (New Living Translation of the Bible) says, 'You are the world's light—a city on a hill, glowing in the night for all to see. Don't hide your light! Let it shine for all!'"

While reflecting on courage, Rollo May affirms that "Courage is not the absence of despair; it is, rather, the capacity to move ahead in spite of despair." Indeed.

CREATE ACHIEVABLE GOALS FOR YOURSELF

A boxing ring is not a place for the timid. Malissa Smith chose to pursue boxing when she was already in her forties, a woman in a still predominantly male sport, without anticipating that the decision would lead her to become one of the world's foremost authorities on women's boxing.

Like Alisa, Malissa had to overcome her fears. But Malissa's perhaps most prescient insights focus on how to hang in there once you have embarked on your dream endeavor.

"Okay, you've started your dream and found the wherewithal to overcome your obstacles, but perhaps it isn't coming as quickly as you might like. Or it might be that you've gone back to school to give yourself the credential to actualize your next step. Learning a sport or the intricacy of a new career takes time, discipline, and a fair amount of patience. What's important is to keep yourself focused on the goals you want to achieve, which might mean giving yourself a series of achievable goals.

I did that with boxing by breaking things down. I'd work on improving stamina for a few months and once that started to improve, I might turn my goal to perfecting a particular punch combination. Just remember, whatever it is will take time."

Malissa understands that progress on any new endeavor takes time; it requires patience and the ability to continuously challenge ourselves by adapting and evolving our goals.

REMEMBER YOU HAVE CHOICES

Caroline de Posada was living out what others expected of her: she became an attorney like her grandfather and was on the path to other people's definition of success. But she had a wild card in her life: her father, Joachim de Posada, a renowned motivational speaker who was untraditional in every sense of the word

Divorced from Caroline's mother, Joachim invited daughter Caroline to travel with him and manage his colorful career. That experience was a catalyst to unlocking a world of possibilities that awakened her soul.

The choices Caroline had made up to that time had served her well, she admits. She adds, "But what made my soul truly come alive were those moments when I got to participate in my dad's world—personal development conferences and workshops, mastermind groups, inspiring conversations, and exchanges of ideas."

When her father passed, "My life as I knew it had died."

Yet, through the sadness, Caroline was energized to follow in her father's footsteps and continue his work. There would be a difference, though. She would walk his path but step into the "shoes of the woman I wanted to be."

"Life is nothing but a series of choices. You do not have to be married to any one path because of a decision made in a previous season. The decisions and choices you make will bring consequences, and those consequences will become part of your new journey."

Today, Caroline is a life coach who helps people with mindset, wellness, and relationships. Her coaching methodology for bridging the gap between where people are and where they want to be puts her lived experience into practice.

"Never forget the power of having a choice," she says. "Choose the next right thing for you—regardless of what others may tell you and despite any doubts about whether or not you're *supposed* to."

– Achim Nowak and Rosemary Ravinal

Essays on Personal Transformation

Roar at the Moon

Dr. Tom Garcia

Tom's close friend Jim was dying. As Tom and his family tended to Jim, Tom faced his own soul wounds and sought escape in the Colorado woods. After Jim's passing, Tom closed his chiropractic practice and emerged as a shamanic healer who serves his clients via transformative fire ceremonies and the creation of community.

On a warm sunny day in early summer, Jim's two sisters arrived at our home. The trees were in full bloom. The sound of kids playing and dogs barking filtered in through an open window. The light in our living room was unusually bright and the wood grain of the ceiling stood out in rich detail. Everything seemed excessively bold and vibrant.

My wife, Carin, and I had invited the sisters over to tell them that we wanted to bring Jim into our home and care for him. They had wanted to put Jim into an assisted living facility, but we were against the idea. We knew it was crazy to even consider taking him in, but Jim had become such a close friend. After his divorce he'd spent so much time with us that he'd become part of our family. We'd seen the changes he was going through and had grown protective of him. There was something else about our decision that was difficult to put into words: It was just the right thing to do. That, and we naively thought we could nurse Jim back to health.

INEXPLICABLE BOND

Jim and I had met a few years before in our men's circle. I had joined the group to help me face my weaknesses without shame and my strengths without arrogance; to be a better father, husband, and mentor. Like me, Jim was in his early 50s and searching for his own answers regarding how to be a whole man in this world. He was laid back with a great sense of humor. We shared common interests.

Both of us were fit and physical. We connected through a mutual love of the outdoors, hiking and climbing the mountains around Durango, Colorado. We forged a friendship over the years that would become what some would call an inexplicable bond between us.

On one trip into the backcountry, the Durango-Silverton train dropped us off in the middle of the wilderness. With full backpacks we began an arduous climb along a thin trail that led to a pristine lake. We spent several days hiking into the surrounding mountains. On the trek back, Jim lagged far behind. When we reached our rendezvous, he lay on the ground exhausted until the train arrived. That was my first inkling that something wasn't right.

Jim's health declined. He started losing his balance and complained of a bad taste in his mouth. The doctors didn't know what was wrong and prescribed medication to treat the symptoms. The side effects made him spacey and lethargic. After several long months with no answers, he was diagnosed with Pick's Disease, a form of dementia similar to Alzheimer's. Jim was relieved to have a diagnosis, but his symptoms progressed until he could no longer live alone.

When Jim walked through his door, no one greeted him. This is why Carin and I needed to bring him into our fold.

THE MESS OF BEING HUMAN

Fast forward three months. Jim's condition worsened. But by then, we knew we would see this journey through to the bitter end.

Every day I showered and shaved Jim. Sometimes during a shave, he'd blurt out, "I love you, Tom."

I'd catch his eye and reply, "I love you too, Jim."

"You missed a spot right here," he'd tell me. The moment of intimacy, of the unabashed affection and good humor between us, would catch me a little off guard. I knew he felt vulnerable and scared. Somehow it had become my job to help him recognize that he was loved and safe; whole and innocent.

Little by little he surrendered, and in turn I surrendered as well.

Jim shared meals with our family and when he could no longer feed himself Carin would feed him, our kids watching. We shared the experience of caring for another human being, and what it meant to communicate unconditional love through every gesture. Even in the mess of being human, there was dignity.

When Jim was no longer able to use a walker, I'd take him out for wheelchair hikes on the trails. When he became confined to bed and couldn't attend our men's circle, we'd set up an empty chair for him. It meant that Jim still had a place in our circle, even if he couldn't physically be with us. There was an unspoken determination amongst us to hold space for him, knowing he was losing ground. The integrity of our circle was strengthened. Each of us knew we belonged, that there was a place for us no matter the circumstances. As a result, we became gentler with each other. A tenderness spilled out everywhere.

A STAKE IN THE GROUND

I'd been searching for deep healing for the better part of my life.

Generations of brokenness and neglect ran rife on both sides of my family (Carin's too). I was born into ancestral trauma, dysfunctional beliefs and behavior. Inherited conversations of unworthiness, scarcity, and lack were my legacy.

There came a point when I knew the time had come for me to do my inner work. On the outside, everything looked good. But beneath my carefully constructed persona, I was dying. The suffering had to end with someone, and that someone was me.

I had a wife and four kids, a mortgage, and a busy chiropractic practice, but I heeded a call.

The day I'd joined the men's circle, I symbolically put a stake in the ground and tied myself to it. I could not know what that declaration would demand from me in the years to come. And part of that demand involved caring for Jim many years later and for reasons I could not foresee at the time.

The sicker Jim got, the more I needed an escape. I began disappearing into the woods before sunrise or at sunset for hours at a time, and then began to stay out all night. Carin would see me pacing restlessly and tell me, "You need to go out." That was all I needed to hear. I'd gather up my gear, my "medicine bag" (an assortment of ceremonial items—sage, a braid of sweetgrass, tobacco, a rattle, feathers, sacred objects for an altar, a special notebook), and head into the woods. There I would make a fire and journal by firelight, sleeping on the earth under an open sky.

One evening our men's group held a fire ceremony for Jim, and as we stood in a circle with our eyes closed, we could hear the crunch of gravel and the rustle of clothing. When I opened my eyes, I saw men, women, and children from our community standing in our circle holding hands. Jim's presence had touched the lives of everyone who had witnessed him yield to the extraordinary love that surrounded him. A love that added immeasurably to the fabric of our community and brought us all closer together.

STARTLED AWAKE

Jim spent the last 18 months of his life with us. He struggled to leave his body and was terrified of letting go. Carin and I were with him right to the end when his labored breathing ceased. We helped him make his transition and together eased his flight into the mystery. There was a moment suspended in time after he passed, the stark realization that he was gone. In the sudden silence we held each other and cried, both of us deeply, profoundly moved.

After Jim passed, we washed and wrapped his body in white linen and colorful sarongs and kept him packed on dry ice for three days while friends and neighbors came and sat quietly in the room with him. During this time, we realized that even in the most difficult moments of those months we felt an abundance of love everywhere around us. Our home was filled with so much light. That light inflamed me.

Life returned to some semblance of normal, except nothing was normal. I would be overcome with emotion at the most inopportune times, sitting in a meeting, working on a patient, or in conversation with a friend. I would cry for no apparent reason, or get angry, or feel unaccountably joyful. The entire experience of caring for Jim and witnessing his withdrawal from life was like being plunged into ice-cold water and startled awake with painful exhilaration to confront my own mortality.

Everything I believed about life and death was turned upside down.

I lost interest in my work and things outside of me. I closed my chiropractic office, walked away from my men's circle, and withdrew from community life. Although I had no words to describe what I was going through, Carin understood even as she worked through her own sense of loss, helpless to do anything about mine.

My life fell apart and everything seemed to unravel.

CRUCIBLE MOMENT

In *Close Encounters of the Third Kind,* Richard Dreyfus' character, possessed by an energy he couldn't fathom, dumped wheelbarrows full of dirt into his living room to make a replica of Devil's Tower. For what reason, he didn't know.

Similarly, I felt driven by an impulse to build beautiful altars and stone fire pits—and make fire. Out of nowhere, I began to crave hot peppers, chili, and spicy food, stoking the fire in my belly.

In early October, several weeks after Jim passed, I went into the woods at dusk. I watched the sun go down and a full moon rise silently in the east. I made a fire and built a crude altar of deer antlers, stones, feathers, shells, and my grandmother's crucifix.

The night was so cold that I practically crawled into the fire to draw heat. I could not get comfortable. I realized that I was grieving and there was no comfort in unexpressed grief. It had been building for weeks. As I moved around the fire, it came out in a torrent of emotion. I roared at the moon. I wanted to tear off my clothes and stand barefoot and naked on the frozen ground and leap into the fire. I bellowed into the night sky, "I am alive! Thank You for my life! Thank You!" and crumbled to my knees in tears.

I'd lost a friend. We walked to the precipice together and he made his transition. I remained with a life to live.

Despite my grief, I felt an overwhelming sense of gratitude for life. All I knew was that I wanted to live. Nothing seemed more important than knowing how to be true to the spirit within me. This was a crucible moment, a turning point that would define the rest of my life.

I also knew in my bones that, beyond the bonds of friendship, Jim and I had shared a sacred contract with one another. Long ago, before we came into this world, we'd agreed that we would find each other and, at the appointed time, help each other to awaken. I would help him find his way out of this life and he would help me find a deeper way in. That was the deal.

I had fulfilled my part, and he would fulfill his.

The fire circle, born of my grief for Jim, would be a work in progress for years to come.

Each week, sometimes several times a week, I would go back into the woods and work on the circle. Many of the rocks were so heavy I called them "penance rocks," because to move them at all was a punishing task. The fire circle became a sacred place on the land, a crude, roughhewn temple of devotion, an outward expression of the altar within my heart. In this sacred fire circle, I would pray for guidance. Later others would join me to engage in the deep work of recovering the memory of who they are.

Meanwhile I was still in the throes of something intangible, unseen. Despite the challenges and difficulties I had experienced up to this point, I felt more alive than ever. I was on the verge of a breakthrough.

What's the point of my life, I wondered. Why am I here? What's my purpose? I wanted to know how to live with integrity and wholeness, how to be true to myself. I wanted a direct experience of the animating Intelligence of the universe. I wanted to know God. Not the God in books or church, or the one I had been conditioned to believe in, or a substitute version that belonged to someone else. The God interpreted by man and contaminated by politics–that God I flatly rejected.

Because a relationship with God, Source of Life, was the only thing that made any sense. That was the healing Presence, the connection, I'd been searching for all along, for as long as I could remember.

STRONG ENOUGH TO HANDLE THE TRUTH

Another full moon came, and the temperature dipped well below freezing. I built a fire and made an altar like before, but more personal and elaborate. The night descended like a shroud, and I knelt at the fire, writing in my journal, waiting—for what I didn't know. Questions that had been swirling in my mind came to life at the fire with such clarity and force that I shouted them aloud.

"I want to know who I am and why I am here.

I want to know who You are and why You sent me to this place.

I want to know!"

Tears came again and something was loosed inside. It felt as though I was being asked to surrender, so I simply surrendered and let go. After a while, my mind became very quiet, and I began to listen intently. In the stillness came a whisper so faint I had to strain to hear anything at all.

"Why are you here?" the whisper asked me.

I didn't have an answer, just tears. "I don't know. Please tell me. I just want the truth."

"Someone has to listen. Pay attention and we will tell you everything. There are no secrets, nothing is hidden. The truth is written everywhere for you to find."

"I'm afraid I'm not doing anybody any good by not telling my truth, the truth of who I am. What is my truth?"

"That's why we brought you to the fire, to listen—for a change. You're not the only one communicating with us, *everything* is. Every living thing has a purpose. You are being guided to yours."

"Where do I begin?"

"Begin by telling the truth of who you are. Your children–they want to know so they can better know themselves. More than anyone else, *you* want to know who you are."

Very gently, the voice spoke through the crackle and pop of the fire, "Open your heart, we are coming through you. We will tell you all you need to know. We made you strong enough to handle the truth."

We went long into the night together in silent conversation. A voice clear and unmistakable, a gentle whisper in the wilderness had come and I dissolved at its sound. I listened and wrote everything it said in my journal.

The voice counseled, "When God talks, take good notes."

I came to know the voice, its timbre and every nuance. This was the connection I'd longed for my entire life. Slowly the truth began to dawn upon my open mind. So began a conversation that would continue uninterrupted for many years to come.

EDGE OF SORROW

Jim's friendship and the ebb of his life was an immense gift catalyzing something completely unexpected within me. It became the story of my awakening, opening a path of unimaginable beauty, exquisite joy, and great challenges. It led to realms beyond the senses and to the dwelling place of the spirit that resides within me. It brought me to the brink of death and life, to the edge of sorrow and surrender.

Immersed in grief, we sometimes lose sight of any associated gift, but if we suspend our grief for a little while, the gift reveals itself. We must ask ourselves, "What is the gift? How does it contribute to our awakening in life?"

Irish poet and playwright, Oscar Wilde, wrote, "Where there is sorrow, there is holy ground."

The ground we stand upon is holy ground because of who we are and what we bring—and because of those who have gone before us.

Everyone who dies leaves behind a gift. We who live are blessed with the task of finding it through our grief. And in the midst of such loss, we may remember our reason for being and appreciate more deeply the life we have been given.

To be alive is to sorrow for something, because the nature of life is one of impermanence, loss, change, transition; in short, death. What dies? What lives?

Letting go allows what is waiting to be born come through us into existence.

SEASON OF AWAKENING

With my friend's passing something awakened in me: an ancient memory, a seed waiting for the right conditions. The ground of our being, like the earth, is fertile soil; the waters of emotion and the light of the spiritual sun within us, all these are the conditions for our transformation. Sometimes it takes decades for us to meet the conditions, but when they are right, when the season of our awakening is upon us, we open, take root and blossom, grateful for the gift.

The ritual of building altars and making fire connected me with nature and the elements. I began to pay more attention to the rising and setting of the sun, the phases of the moon, and the movement of stars in the sky. I felt a visceral connection to my ancestors—the ancient ones—and beings who lived on the land, in the woods. These were things not easily explained, but I felt guided and protected in pursuit of understanding the underlying reality of all things and the deeper meaning of life itself.

A ceremony, ancient and primal, came up from the earth and out of the fire. It came through me, a sacred gift from my ancestors, a way to offer prayers and blessings, express gratitude; a place to lay down the accumulated detritus—the burdens—of daily life. I was grateful for the salvaging of my mind and spirit. The voice that came to me and the fire ceremony that came through me changed the course of my life and gave me a way to help others on their path.

There was a time when I was afraid the voice would leave me, that one day I would wake up, the voice would be gone, and with it the ceremony, the fire, and my connection. Instead, the voice became stronger and clearer. I came to know the sound of the voice the way a child knows the sound of his mother's voice and listens for it.

Early in our conversations the voice told me that the messages I received were not just for me alone. They must be shared. But I hesitated, not yet feeling strong enough in my faith. I was afraid to be so vulnerable and exposed, not sure I could trust myself to share what had been given me. The voice would gently say, "When you are ready." And then add, "We have an eternity to wait, but you don't."

RECLAIM THE SACRED

In the months and years that followed, the voice spoke quietly of things I struggled with and led me to heal the places where I felt inadequate, unworthy and afraid, and helped me to heal the relationships with those closest to me. This is what I had been after all along. This is what had led me to the very circle where Jim and I had met.

When I would falter, the voice would gently whisper, "Don't be afraid, just listen."

The voice told me that prayer was its language and that this was how it communicated with me.

"Pray in your own words, out loud, so we can hear you."

And often it would say, "Laugh more, because we like the sound."

It took the first 50 years of my life before my ceremony found me, and another 10 years to truly make it mine. These last several years have been a time of deeper trust and surrender to discover my real work. To discover the sacred vessel that I am and was always meant to be. Even in the earliest days, as I knelt at the fire listening, the voice told me, "Help them find their way."

I now understand that in helping others find their way, I find my own way.

Over the years I have facilitated hundreds of ceremonial fires that heal and bless and help others come into the light of their own wisdom and to apprehend what is most sacred in their lives. The fire that lives in each of us is sacred, as we are. For many of us, our work is to reclaim the sacred, take back our true identity, and live with gusto.

Dr. Tom Garcia is a soul-centered coach and transformational guide. His calling is to teach, lead, and guide people to awaken to their higher purpose so that they live healthier, happier, and more fulfilling lives.

My Road to Healing

Mark J. Silverman

Mark Silverman went from being homeless to becoming a millionaire to losing it all again. Mark's life kept falling apart, and he felt powerless to stop the falling. His journey into personal healing, Mark learned, was a journey into more fully and more resoundingly knowing self-love.

> Things falling apart is a kind of testing and also a kind of healing. We think that the point is to pass the test or to overcome the problem, but the truth is that things don't really get solved. They come together and they fall apart. Then they come together again and fall apart again. It's just like that. The healing comes from letting there be room for all of this to happen: room for grief, for relief, for misery, for joy.
>
> Pema Chödrön, *When Things Fall Apart: Heart Advice for Difficult Times*

I come at success from a different perspective.

September 1, 1989. Twenty-seven years old, weighing all of 135 pounds, I rolled into Washington, DC in my little red Toyota pickup, which is where I'm living at the time. I had been driving around the country, surviving on maxed-out credit cards, and I was in town to borrow money from my older brother, who owned several successful restaurants.

I had been homeless.

My brother graciously took me in, on the condition that I attend Alcoholics Anonymous and Narcotics Anonymous, enroll in community college, and join him at the gym. This was the beginning of my journey to sobriety, health, and growing up.

Several years later, I was a millionaire, married with two kids, driving a brand-new Lexus. I was great at sales. The joke I start many of my talks with is, "I'm basically a short, Jewish Tony Robbins."

Running away from my past, I chased perfection. I was all things to all people, outworking those around me. Someone once remarked, "If you walk into a room, half the people will like you and half the people will not. Mark is different. Everyone likes Mark." That was by desperate design.

WHEN THINGS KEPT FALLING APART

While I pedaled as fast as I could in the world, inside I had crippling fear and self-loathing. I felt small and ill-equipped in a big, scary world. The shiny outside gave way to the deep cracks making their way to the surface.

Two decades after getting sober and creating the dream life I had always wanted, things changed. My marriage fell apart. Sales dried up, and my career was sinking fast. Panic attacks were a daily occurrence.

I remember walking off the elevator at a customer site and running into the CIO I had worked with for years.

"Hi Mark."

I couldn't answer. There was no air in my lungs, and nothing came out. We just looked at each other for what seemed like an eternity before I could squeak, "Hey Dan."

I would break out in hives at high-profile meetings and run out the door before they became too visible. Dramatic weight loss and unexpected illnesses were becoming my new reality. I couldn't understand how this was happening, *stone cold sober.*

It seemed like one minute I was a successful business and family man, committee chair for the Boy Scouts, and third-grade basketball coach, and the next minute I was sitting in the wreckage of my life. I felt humiliated. I felt that everyone could see me for the loser I really was. My past had caught up to me.

It wasn't until much later that I could see it. The person I was inside could not sustain all that I had built on the outside. I was living a slow-motion crash that I couldn't stop. The sad irony was that the wreckage felt more familiar, more comfortable than the success. *It felt like what I deserved.*

All I could do was walk. During the day, when the panic set in at the office, I would head outside and stride around the business park until I could calm down enough to go back to my desk. Nights were even more horrible. The pain in my body was so acute that I would pace by my window hoping a stray bullet would find me.

I would wake up at 2 a.m. and hit the sidewalk. The town would be empty, and I would walk for miles until I was exhausted enough to go back to bed.

I wanted to die, but I knew I couldn't kill myself. I would not leave that burden on my children.

The doctors did not know what was wrong with me, misdiagnosing me several times. I was so sick that I was sure I was going to die within the year.

THE TURNING POINT

In the parking lot, as I was waiting on yet another doctor's appointment, I heard an interview with champion ultramarathon runner, Stu Mittleman. He said, "Everyone can run. It is what we humans are built to do." And I believed him.

That was my spark.

I made a decision. If I was going to die, I was going to leave a legacy for my ex-wife and kids.

My goal for that year was:

- Run the Marine Corps Marathon (even though I couldn't run a mile).
- Make $1 million to leave behind for my family.
- Give $60,000, the amount the insurance had paid out for my medical bills, to charity because I didn't feel deserving.

I called Stu Mittleman and asked him to coach me. He agreed but said it would take 18 months to be ready for the marathon. I told him I had to do it in eight months because I was not sure I'd be around for the next marathon.

At the same time, a friend called and asked me to join his new startup. I was drowning at my current job, so this was an opportunity to start over. Of course, I knew I would fail, destroy another friendship, and humiliate myself, but I needed an escape. I needed to buy time.

In 2009, I ran the Marine Corps Marathon, finishing an hour faster than my best practice time. It had taken me a year and a half, but I made the million dollars. On December 31st, I wrote the last check to charity, bringing my total contributions to more than $60,000. I had achieved my goals.

I was now healthier than I had ever been, my career was soaring, and my family was healing.

So now what? Finances were back on track. The panic attacks and hives were gone…. And I still wanted to die.

Unrelenting self-hatred greeted me every morning and waited for me in the evening. There was no escape.

THE CLIMB

Training for the marathon took many hours per week. During my training, I listened to numerous self-help and spiritual books. Brian Johnson's A *Philosopher's Notes* (summaries of the greatest books ever written) became my saving grace. I wanted to die… and, in those fortuitous audios, I found a spark of possibility.

My new friends were Steve Chandler, Martin Seligman, Sonja Lyubomirsky, Ram Dass, Thich Nhat Hanh, the Stoics, Mahatma Gandhi, among others.

Commitment to my responsibility as a father pulled me through the worst of it. While my children were still at home, I never lived more than walking distance away from my former family home. It was that commitment that had me dig deep to find a way to live so that I could raise my sons properly. My family (including my ex) was everything.

I did not expect to ever enjoy life again, but I was going to be the best I could be for those who depended on me. I studied ferociously. Ancient wisdom, positive psychology, anything that would give me an insight, a tool, or some hope. I highly recommend one especially helpful resource: Pema Chödrön's *When Things Fall Apart: Heart Advice for Difficult Times.*

TRANSFORMATION CAME SLOWLY

The change was so slow I barely noticed any movement. It is only in hindsight that I could see it.

- Year 1: I decided to live until my youngest graduated high school.
- Year 2: I felt like I could go on.
- Year 3: I was kind of enjoying life…when I forgot to hate it.
- Year 4: I was doing ok.
- Year 5: I crossed a threshold.

I had started a deep meditation and journaling practice, and my consumption of "good stuff" remained at a fever pitch. Brian Johnson, the author I mentioned above, said that he studied and worked hard at growth in order to outrun depression. I totally related.

Sai Baba, a loving and brilliant Indian guru, taught that breakthrough is like trying to crack a rock. You tap and tap with little progress. Then one day, you tap and everything changes. Every one of those taps contributes to the moment of breakthrough.

My fateful tap came from the author, Alan Cohen. One day I was reading Alan's *Relax Into Wealth*. This sentence jumped out at me:

What if you treated yourself the way you treat everyone else in your life?

I wasn't even sure the question was in English; it was that foreign a concept to me.

I looked around my apartment at my $7 IKEA tables, mismatched silverware, and old plates. I couldn't let myself furnish my new life. I deserved nothing. Everything went to my family.

Depriving myself felt like the exact right thing to balance the crushing guilt.

One night while I was putting my son to bed, he looked up at me and said, "I don't even remember you living here anymore." It was a knife to my heart. I suddenly realized how far to the margin I'd pushed myself. How could I ever forgive myself, let alone treat myself like a person?

My ex and the kids lived in our paid-off, million-dollar house. I had purchased them a brand-new SUV (so they would be safe), a baby grand piano (encouraging my ex to start playing again), a new couch, and a big-screen TV. I had even encouraged my ex to renovate the kitchen and her bedroom so she could feel better about life.

Treat myself like I treat them? Blasphemy! Impossible! Irresponsible!

This new thought wouldn't leave me. I meditated on it. I journaled exhaustively.

Something shifted while journaling one morning. My hand wrote, "I was once an innocent, precious, perfect child…just like my kids. Maybe, just maybe, I have… worth. Maybe."

I stared at the page. Often when I journal, something will emerge from my pen that seems to have come from someone or somewhere else.

I tried this new concept on for size. I started with my living space. I bought a leather couch and a really nice TV. That felt good, so I bought an entire cherry bedroom set. I was making a home.

With my ex's encouragement, I bought my dream car, a sonic blue Lexus convertible. "You work so hard for everyone, you deserve something nice," she said.

The "stuff" was nice. Then something incredible happened when I allowed Alan Cohen's words to integrate. I had been happy to move from *wanting to die*, to being *ok to live*. Even this exceeded my expectations. Could I hope for more?

What if I treated myself with love and compassion, the way I treat everyone else in my life?

What if I stopped trashing myself at every turn? What if I actually got on my own side? What if I actually...loved myself?

And there it was. The light I never knew existed. I could love myself. I had worth. Value.

SHOUTING FROM THE ROOFTOPS

The joy was immeasurable. I wanted to shake everyone I met.... "YOU HAVE WORTH. YOU ARE LOVED!"

I have dedicated my life to sharing this one small but mighty insight. I wish I could say it is a permanent shift. That I never slip into self-criticism or despair. I do. But not that often and not for long.

THE NOT-SO-SECRET INGREDIENT

Sitting on my meditation cushion, I am filled with gratitude. Thankful for the way my life has turned out. Thankful that my sons have grown to be amazing young men. Thankful that I get to make a difference in the world every day.

> G-d, thank you for choosing me for this work, in spite of all my glaring shortcomings.

The response boomed from everywhere all at once....

> I chose you BECAUSE of your shortcomings!

Whatever your story, you can change it. The past does not define you.

Your experiences can fuel your gift to the world, if you choose to make it so.

If you're going through hell, just keep going until the gold reveals itself.

Mark J. Silverman is an executive coach, speaker, and the host of "The Rising Leader Podcast." His bestselling book, *Only 10s 2.0: Confront Your To-Do List and Transform Your Life* has sold over 75,000 copies to date.

When I Was Willing
To Try Anything

Achim Nowak

When 33-year-old theater director Achim Nowak was told he had at best a few years left to live, he checked himself into a healing center in the Arizona desert to heal his body. He received a spiritual awakening instead—and 6 months later, he left his life in Manhattan to live on the small island of Tobago where he became a windsurfer.

1989 rushed in like the nor'easter you wished had never come. I had been told in the final week of 1988 that I had tested HIV-positive. My T4 cell count—then widely considered the indicator of the body's immune health—had dropped below 200. And it was plummeting with each new round of bloodwork. Below 200—that, according to the experts, was the death zone. It made me an instant candidate for every opportunistic infection associated with AIDS. PCP. Karposi's sarcoma. Swollen glands. Swollen feet, swollen everything. I was 33 years old.

Dr. Howard Grossman, my physician of the moment, a preeminent AIDS expert in Manhattan, sat me down in his basement office on East 29th Street. "Expect to be in the hospital within two years," he announced with a somber voice and serious-doctor demeanor. "That'll be the beginning of the end."

Well, it was a heck of a lot more affirming to hang out with the urine drinkers at the Water of Life support group on West Thirteenth Street. We studied poorly mimeographed sheets of esoteric pamphlets that touted the benefits of drinking our own urine, as practiced in India. We compared our urine-drinking techniques. First thing in the morning, every day, I stood at my bathroom sink, my cock in one hand, a glass in the other. Spilled the first part of my piss; that was the poisonous part, I had been told. Caught the middle shoot in the glass. Shook it and then chugged it. My morning cocktail.

Twice a week I took the Number 6 train up to the South Bronx. Got off at Brook Avenue and marched through blocks and blocks of housing projects to a drug rehab clinic where Frankie Lipman, a young physician from South Africa, gave free acupuncture treatments to positives like me. I plunged myself into the books of Louise Hay, who claims that every physical illness is the manifestation of a deeper psychic imbalance that needs to be healed. Went to the Louise Hay healing circles in a little second-story walk-up on West Fourteenth Street, every Thursday evening at 8, and spent hours hugging people I had not met before.

Mind you, this is not a tale of how I survived HIV. I have no definitive insights for you. Don't know why I'm alive and why Joe, the architect who lived across the street from me, isn't. Cannot explain why my friend Anthony, the choreographer, spent four years bouncing in and out of Cabrini Hospital with immune infections and I didn't. I simply don't know. But in those weeks and months, when every waking moment of my life was consumed with tending to my physical self, I was offered a sudden glimpse of an entirely different world. Nothing afterward would ever be the same.

OFF TO THE DESERT I GO

Toward the end of '89, the year when I was willing to try anything, Dr. Grossman suggested I take AZT. It was the only HIV drug available in the late 80s and highly toxic. When I refused, Dr. Grossman declared that I was in a state of denial and should see a therapist at once.

I went to the desert instead.

On a blustery Sunday afternoon in November, I found myself lying flat on my back on a stone ledge atop an old Anasazi burial mound in Arizona. It was the Sunday before Thanksgiving, and even in the desert a thin sheet of frost had sealed the earth. Listening to a Kitaro tape on my Walkman and feeling the brisk wind bite my cheeks, I glanced up at the vast Navajo sky and wondered how the hell I had ended up here.

The evening before, I had settled into my room at the Golden Phoenix, just outside the village of Rimrock, halfway up Highway 17 in the direction of Sedona. The Phoenix looked exactly like the abandoned dude ranch that it was, dusty and barren and utterly lacking in charm. It wrapped itself around the burial mound where I now lay. A house sat on top of this mound but that is not where we actually lived. The house atop the mound was a ruin. The desert wind whipped and howled through its cracked window panes.

Two small houses sat on a promontory, midway down the slope. They had a new, prefabricated look, although they, too, seemed to seep into the dust of the earth. That's where the patients roomed.

By the end of this first night, we had dubbed our quarters AIDS Camp. There were eight of us. I was the only one without symptoms. We had all come to Arizona for the same reason. Word in the New York underground was that positives were turning negative, and the Golden Phoenix was the place to make it happen.

Reverend Mona didn't show up for another five days. Maybe it was because my mind had already started to drift. Maybe it was simply the phosphorescent desert light–but Mona didn't look well. Mona was just a little past fifty and had run through four husbands. It showed. Her eyes were lined with bags the color and size of small chestnuts, permanently etched under her lower lids. The porcupine hair, a blend of dark roots and infinite shades of peroxide, had not been washed in days.

Mona was recuperating from a cold that didn't want to quit. She sat on a chair at the far end of the kitchen table, clutched a crumpled paper tissue, sucked rot up her nose. Mona chain-smoked. She didn't smoke in the kitchen that afternoon, never in front of the guests in fact, but I smelled a wave of stale nicotine breath. I glanced at her as she slumped into her kitchen chair and felt a wrench turn my stomach. This woman looked like a car wreck, like a major highway collision beyond repair. And Mona *was* the Golden Phoenix. She was the reason I had come.

Mona disappeared again for the rest of the week. It was just as well. I wanted hope, not Mona, not this.

In the meantime, she had put us all on a deprivation detox. Pump the insides clean before you rebuild them, that was Mona's approach to healing the body. Every two hours I drank a juice. In between juices I popped pills. I wish I could tell you every little ingredient that was in the juices, and give you the list of the pill cocktails I swallowed in those days. Truth is, it all happened over thirty years ago, and I plain don't remember. I know that I threw myself into this structure with a desperate commitment. Because a routine was something I could hold onto. It was the one predictable feature in a life where nothing was predictable anymore.

Niacin provided the only twitch of excitement. It was one of the pills that I took every day. It sent me into an instant red swirl. My skin erupted into little fires that rushed to every cell of my body, it seemed. They prickled and flamed. We all called it the niacin rush. It lasted a few minutes only, but I began to look forward to the niacin now. It was the one surefire thrill in this numbing routine.

The little nourishment I took in I flushed out again, twice a day, when I did my enemas. Rob and I started to throw enema parties, because it was just too boring to do an enema alone, day in and day out. Rob was my roommate and the jock in this group, the former model, the Wall Street lawyer. His frame had shrunk by sixty pounds this year, he told me. He was slender where he had been beefed up before and still so very beautiful, but that he didn't seem to know. His lover, the famous dancer, had left him months ago. Rob was a few weeks shy of thirty.

Rob and I spread a plastic trash bag on the bathroom floor, because you never knew when you were going to spill. Greased the plastic spouts and then stuck the tubes up our butts, all the way into the rectum, as far as they would go. Then we slid our naked legs right up against the wall, nested the heels into the towel rack.

Rob's butt rested next to mine, and with him beside me the enema protocol suddenly became a game we played. Who would hold the spout the entire fifteen minutes? Who would persevere, who would clean out the most? We ended with separate dumps, and I looked closely each time at what had landed in the toilet bowl–the small ringlets and squiggles of shit that reconfigured every day, the dribbles of blood that circled the water, the fields of mucus that floated around my excretion, like lava from a volcanic eruption.

THE VISIONS COME

Irony has it, as my body began to clear out, I started to see things. The first vision came one morning, unannounced. I was on one of my juice breaks and wandered down to the brook that ran along the base of the hill. The water was clear and cool, and I planted my feet firmly in the riverbed. I stood right at the bend where the brook formed a little tub in the earth. My feet curved into the soft river mud and my eyes looked west to the corroding fence of another horse ranch, when suddenly they appeared–a peacock, a bear, an eagle, and a deer. They flashed for a moment, sharp and very clear, across the morning sky, then vanished. The eagle reappeared on my head, the peacock walked toward me through the water, the deer and the bear stood on opposite banks of the river and watched.

This moment shivered across the brook but I, of course, felt it shiver right down my spine. The desert was starting to inhabit my brain. The juices and the enemas were sucking my intestines dry, and the walks in the brisk mountain wind were pinching my nerves. This moment excited me and frightened me, all at once. It frightened me because I couldn't question it. It had happened, and I could not wish it away.

When I returned to the hill I didn't tell Rob, didn't tell anyone what I had seen. The animals, they were my little secret. And they came to visit me every day now. Late at night, when the moon skimmed over the porch swing and Rob heaved heavy in his pillow, in the shower as the hot water drummed my chest, in the morning during morning meditation when I did the Hu-Hus.

The Hu-Hus–that's where we jumped in place with our eyes shut tight and our hands pressed high into the air, palms flat as if they were holding up the sky. I didn't know jumping could hurt like this.

My body ached with each bounce, my arms wanted to fall limp with exhaustion. The push toward the sky, the drop into the floor; they seemed to unravel my knotted spine. And with each jump I let out a sound, it sort of sounded like *hu-hu*. I was sure of it: The Hu-Hus were my wake-up call, and they were hurtling me into a visionary world.

I ran back to the river every day now. There was one place I loved above all the others. It's where the leopard came to visit me. I raced down the hill and crossed a mud-caked plateau, flung aside hip-high shrubs that broke at a touch. Then I stepped over a much-stepped-over chicken-wire fence and descended into a narrow gorge. There was no water there anymore, and the earth in the gorge was dry. I pressed my back into the pebbled ground, wiggled it until the fit was snug. When I looked up I saw the split trunk of a tree, and branches that looped into spirals, and beyond it the vaulting sky.

The second I closed my eyes he came. He always came alone. I lay with my eyes shut and felt the leopard rise from my crotch. He climbed on top of my chest, sat and sprawled and then covered the entire length of my body. He was not an image in my mind, no, this leopard had form and weight, a lot of weight, his energy shot straight into my limbs, pressed into me fast–it was a hot, surging kind of energy. My limbs quivered and fell with the force of his weight. I felt my flesh and my bones drop away, as if the leopard's belly were crushing me into the earth. I felt his hot breath sweep over my face. It was a breath of fire and rot and sweet, dangerous life. Leaves rustled and drubbed my face, and the weight seemed to shove me deeper and deeper into the earth. I felt the hot desert wind sweep over me, and then, suddenly, I was swallowed into the ground.

When I opened my eyes I saw the sky again. It suddenly seemed even more distant and vast and so brilliantly clear. My body brimmed with a keen, racing energy. I was very confused. I lay so still here in this gorge, yet this is exactly what it felt like: I was in the middle of a race. My entire body was charging forward, to a world I had not known before.

MONA KNOWS

A week or so passed. I was no longer sure of the day, just as I was sure of little else. But every time I returned from one of my trips to the gorge the urge got stronger: I had to tell someone. I had to tell them that I was losing touch with … with what, I didn't know.

One afternoon, as I stepped out of the kitchen door, I noticed Mona. She was sitting in the old Impala that was parked off to one side of the shack, having a smoke. Mona looked like a little schoolgirl who had squeezed into a toilet stall, afraid to be caught. I swallowed a whiff of the desert air, gulped, and then I slipped into the ripped car seat beside her.

Mona looked at me with a quizzical frown. I was terrified. I was convinced Mona knew that I thought she was a total quack. A smirk settled on her lips, and she listened impassively as I began to tell her about my moment in the brook. I told her everything. I spoke so fast that I don't believe I caught a single breath. Right after I stopped talking my chest unfurled, and then the silence in the car threatened to implode. Finally, Mona's mouth stretched to smile.

"Welcome," she said.

I had not yet studied the Native American Medicine Wheel or the symbolic meaning of Power Animals or the role of shape-shifters. Had not read *Black Elk Speaks* or *I Send A Voice* or any of the other books that would help me to appreciate the mystery of the spirit world in the years to come. "Welcome." That was all I needed that day. I trembled as I heard Mona say the word. It was as if she had given me instant permission to enter this new world.

I ran down to the brook and my gorge every day now, three, four, five times a day. Suddenly I felt as if my day was split in half. My life on the mound with its body rituals–the drinks, the pills, the enemas. My life down by the river, deep in the dusty plain. And my doubts began to disappear. I was living on a burial mound, after all, and the spirit world was calling me.

EXTREME MEASURES

"It's time to stop the bullshit," Mona declared a few weeks later over lunch. The sky outside was drooping in thick, gray lumps. Mona sat in a corner and leaned into the kitchen table and looked irritatingly perky as she sucked on a cherry pit. "Time to do the Intensive," Mona said.

I still wanted to cling to the belief that my visit here was all about my body. Wanted to cleanse and dump and cleanse and dump and be done. The Intensive–that's where Mona messed with all the other stuff that lived somewhere inside. Energy. Rage. Pain. Spirit. It was all the stuff I really didn't understand.

Late in the first night of the Intensive, Mona took all eight of us into the kitchen and fed us each a large bowl of ice cream. The ice cream landed on the shores of my cleansed stomach like the eye of a tornado. That, I realized, was Mona's intent. Because right afterward I stood in the darkened garage next to the stables and yelled invectives into a plastic bag. Mona dared us to yell loud and hard. Phlegm and vomit and blood spewed from my mouth. Spit flung to the floor. I aimed for the plastic bag between my legs but missed. I was losing my aim, so I just yelled louder. It came out easily now. Froth dripped from my lips, rot smeared my chin, it fell, and I wondered, where was this all coming from, where? All around me others were yelling just as loud. Waves and waves of more rage shot up my throat, spat into the bag. And I just pushed and pushed it out, screamed and screamed and vomited.

That night, as I stumbled from the garage back to my room, I felt as if I no longer existed. My flashlight cut a narrow path up the hill. The night wind howled and creaked. Rob's arm hung on mine. He pressed his chest into my shoulder and wrapped himself around my neck. I watched his breath as it escaped into the night, and yet all I felt was the absolute absence of any weight.

"Time to stop the bullshit," Mona said every morning now. These were the days of playing games. Lifeboat. I Love You Enough To Tell You the Truth About Yourself As I See It. Games of confrontation with who we pretended to be. Games about the empty roles we played, even here at the Phoenix. "Time to stop the bullshit." Mona said it with such a vile sound of disgust that I suddenly wondered, was she playacting, or was this contempt for real?

"One more game," Mona said one morning. "This is it."

WHEN THE BULLSHIT STOPPED

The rules were simple. I would lie on my bed, for several days and nights, for an unspecified amount of time. I didn't know how long because Mona wouldn't say. My eyes would be blindfolded, my room shuttered dark. When I raised my hand. Mona would come and take me to the bathroom. When she tapped me on the shoulder, she would bring food or drink. There was no other contact with anyone.

The second I slipped on my blindfold I entered the longest night of my life. Long because there really was no end in sight. Mona had shut off every emergency exit. My physical world had suddenly shrunk. From the desert and the plains I'd visited daily, to the narrow borders of my cot. I lay in silence, but it was an outer silence only. The animals were back, and they all seemed to live in my body now. I felt spiders climb my thighs. Ants marched down my chest, they pricked my skin like tiny burning needles. Flies seemed to settle on my forehead and walk on my brain. Yes, it was a jungle in here.

I had many visions that night. They came right after I entered the darkness. Sometimes life is a cliché. This was one of those moments. The night was the operator. It pushed the button, and in my mind a screen appeared. Literally so. The film rolled. There was nothing I could do to stop it. No off switch, no brake. Memory had a very specific location that night. It sat right there on that screen in my forehead and unfurled with relentless alacrity. Moments chase other moments as if there isn't enough time to see them all. I was on that screen, I was in every frame, but my eyes stood outside and watched. I became the witness in a race to my past.

The memories weren't random. No, they were the memories of every person my body had loved, slept with, abandoned. I was surprised at how many of these moments there were. They chased each other in a rapid-fire assault, and each was so stunningly empty. I lay on my cot in a delirious quiver. It was not an unpleasant sensation, and it was void of any sort of pain, marked only by a startling clarity. I saw the distances between the people on the screen. They loomed so very large, these distances, and they began to obliterate all other details of memory. Each memory was a moment of distance. Each memory was the memory of a person alone.

When the memories stopped, I completely fell out of the screen, and now it became a screen of only color and shape. I suddenly watched corners appear, as if they were rising straight out of the earth. The entire screen turned into a maze of corners and walls that extended further and further into the distance. My maze shimmered in a brilliant light, it seemed to oscillate at every turn, and suddenly light ripped like a fire across the screen, it cut and burned right through these walls until it erased every incident, every memory, simply everything, and then I saw nothing but a field of clear, undulating light.

When the film came to an end, and it did, I don't know how many minutes, hours later, I turned over into my bed and curled in. It felt like a collapse, yet I had collapsed before, and no collapse had ever felt like this, and how could I collapse when there was nothing to collapse into, but that is exactly what it felt like. I folded into the sheet on which I lay, and my bed became the ocean where I drowned.

I longed for the moments when Mona came. The moments when I felt her hand tap my arm. I rose on the cot and reached into the darkness, felt the rim of a bowl with food, felt her hand for a short second. The rough, warm touch of her skin jolted my body like the charge of an electrical current. I wanted her hand to linger, didn't want it to leave at all. These were the moments when I completely surrendered to her. It was quite simple, I really had no choice.

The hours of darkness filled me with many more visions. They came suddenly and very fast. One stood out from all the others.

Toward the very end of this night in my room, just before Mona released me from my cot, a small white house appeared on my screen. It sat alone on a dense, dark green mountain slope. The vegetation on this slope was tropical and lush. I knew, as I looked at this house, that it was an island house. It crested high above a shimmering, dark sea. A brilliant speck of white dropped into a field of deep green, suspended in midair between a scintillating sky and the black-blue ocean. I had never even thought of going to the islands. But I knew at once that this house was not a metaphor, it was a very specific place. And I knew I would have to go there.

Two and a half days later, when Mona removed the blindfold, I saw a room that had changed. The light lacerated, its flicker was so bright, so unrelenting. The wall, the door, the floor, Mona, everything around me vibrated. I stood in a pulsing, vibrating room. The light outside was even brighter, its ferocity so unbearable, I had to shield my face. Only when I stepped into the bathroom and looked at myself in the mirror did the vibrating stop. Instantly. I was startled. I didn't recognize myself. The difference was in the eyes. They were clear.

"You looked so still on your cot," Mona said to me as I stepped back into the hallway, "like you had died."

EPILOGUE

I left the Golden Phoenix a week before Christmas, 1989. When Dr. Grossman did my next round of bloodwork, he was startled. My T4 cells had doubled. Rob and the others who had stayed with me during my six weeks at the Phoenix, they all passed away within the next twelve months. I'm the only one who survived. I went to the memorial services. I celebrated, I cried. And yet, as one by one my friends were dying, I somehow no longer believed that this was really all about the body.

I left my life as a professional theater director in New York. Became a mediator who worked on conflict resolution projects in the Middle East for Seeds of Peace and the Shimon Peres Center for Peace and Innovation. Wrote some books. Started a firm. Coached highly successful business executives in every part of the world. And within six months of leaving the Golden Phoenix, I moved into a little white house atop a cliff, on the island of Tobago, overlooking the Atlantic, and became a windsurfer.

One evening, as I sat on the terrace of my Tobago house and watched moonlight sprinkle the Atlantic, I remembered a walk I'd taken at the Golden Phoenix. When I had marched into the desert in between my juice times, I usually went alone. Once in a while I took Douglas. He lived in the main house where Mona put the severe cases. Douglas had survived PCP, the serious AIDS pneumonia, six times. Nobody was supposed to survive PCP more than once. This last summer Douglas had lost his sight.

I picked Douglas up from his bed and guided him sideways past the narrow open space between the kitchen counter and the supply closet, out the front door. Here Douglas folded his arm into mine, as if we were going for a formal promenade. Then we walked slowly down the gravel road that curved around the mound and headed into the plains. Douglas's body was slender but not frail, his skin very soft, like that of a little boy. His head turned toward me with exquisite grace, as if to make sure he didn't miss a word I said. Last time Douglas had been at the Golden Phoenix he could still see. So he knew the landscape I described to him.

We ended up on a muddy plateau where our trail suddenly vanished. A chicken-wire fence stretched into the distance and separated one empty plain from another. Here we stood still for a moment. The quiet here in the plains was hollow and cold.

"Why do you keep going?" I asked Douglas. My body trembled as I looked straight at his eyes. "Why are you still here?"

"I don't know," Douglas shrugged with a measured calm. "I don't know."

And then, as if it were an afterthought, he announced: "I dumped my boyfriend this summer."

I want to say there was an absence of will as he spoke, but no, I watched Douglas's chin jut forward with a proud determination. I had not expected his defiance.

"Why?" I wanted to know.

"Because he didn't love me anymore."

Achim Nowak is an executive coach, podcaster, TEDx speaker and the author of three books on personal excellence. His writing has been published in numerous anthologies and received a PEN Syndicated Fiction Award.

Reflections on Personal Transformation

"There can be no rebirth without a dark night of the soul," wrote Inayat Khan, the father of modern Sufism, "a total annihilation of all you believed in and thought you were." American mythologist Joseph Campbell, who popularized the theory of the archetypal hero's journey, explains: "The dark night of the soul comes just before revelation. When everything is lost, and all seems darkness, then comes the new life and all that is needed."

The three authors in this section of *The Difference* experienced their version of a dark night in which an old Self, with its attachments and illusions, dies. The sudden death of someone we love, the end of a relationship we thought would last forever, a climate catastrophe, an act of war, a health scare—they all can become the catalyst that sends us into a dark night.

Does something tragic have to occur before we have an awakening? Does our life need to "hit bottom," to use language from the 12-step recovery world? Or is it possible to actively initiate such a deeply personal transformation? Here is what our three authors discovered.

HEAR THE VOICE THAT LONGS TO GUIDE YOU

As Dr. Tom Garcia accompanied his friend Jim on Jim's journey into death, Tom was almost unwittingly drawn into his own dark night of the soul. It pulled him from a life he had outgrown—that of a successful chiropractor—to the life of a healer who is deeply connected to the wisdom and energy of the elements.

Tom writes powerfully about "hearing the voice" and heeding the call to reclaim the sacred. He exhorts all of us to listen to the voices in our lives that are calling us toward our own awakening.

"You are never alone," Tom assures us. "Whatever your struggle, you are always guided and protected, surrounded by light. No call for help goes unanswered. Remember this, especially in moments of difficulty and despair. Your prayers are always answered. Look for signs, and when you see a sign, take it! Trust your inner guidance and follow where it leads you."

Tom emphasizes that personal transformation begins with our desire to hear the voice. "There is a voice that speaks your name; listen for it without strain. We all have a voice, but you must still your mind and surrender yourself to it. Call it the Holy Spirit, Higher Self, your Inner Being. Name it whatever you want! Just remember to ask for its guidance in all matters. If you cannot hear the voice, it is because you have chosen not to listen."

SEEK OUT GUIDANCE IN ITS MANY FORMS

Mark Silverman's journey through his dark night feels a bit like being inside the movie *Groundhog Day*. The same patterns, the same experiences keep replaying themselves, again and again, until Mark learns to trust a more deeply known self-love.

Mark's turning point began with his voracious absorption of positive, life-affirming writing and thought. He reminds us that his affirmation of self-worth was, and is, nurtured by very specific practices: "It still takes work. All the things that brought me to the revelation of my self-worth are things I practice every day." Mark recommends these elements of his daily routine.

- Consume uplifting and inspiring content.
- Embrace service as a way of life—and a way to get out of yourself.
- Practice not believing your thoughts.
- Find a contemplation practice, like journaling or meditation.

While the above practices were the foundation of creating a life worth living, Mark emphasizes that, by themselves, they were not sufficient for him to make his shift. "The difference came from a decision. I had to decide, and still do in each moment, to love myself. Despite all the evidence I have that I am a 'worthy person,' I must:

- Choose to be worthy.
- Choose to be lovable.
- Choose to create a life worth living."

Mark leaves us with this compelling affirmation: "You are already all of these things. Worthy. Lovable. Possessed of a life worth living. Might as well accept it."

DISRUPT EVERYTHING

When I, Achim, was told I had a few years left to live before my body would start to decay and die, I entered the first phase of my dark night. This prediction emboldened me to experiment with my health and take risks I might otherwise not have considered. It dared me to leave behind the familiar confines of my world and spend six weeks in an esoteric retreat center.

At this center, the spiritual leader initiated a very literal dark night when she blindfolded me and banished me to the confines of a small cot. Reverend Mona removed all escape routes for me. She "made me" go into the dark night of my soul.

In hindsight, I know that what Mona created for me on that cot was a vision quest. Many native cultures in the Americas, and around the planet, venerate the experience of a vision quest. It is a rite of passage where teenagers go into the wilderness, often for multiple days, leave behind the world they know, and receive visions, wisdom, and guidance from Spirit.

If the notion of going on a vision quest speaks to you, do some research. You will find tribal communities and organizations that host vision quests, or modern adaptations of ancient vision quest traditions.

Here's what you can do on your own: Dislocate yourself. Live for a while in a place far away from where you currently reside, away from the people you know.

Getting an HIV+ diagnosis was not a dislocation I chose. Going to the Arizona desert was. So was living in Tobago, an island that prior to my stay in Arizona I would not have been able to find on a map. In Tobago, I learned other soul lessons that I could only learn there. Such is the transformative power of dislocation.

While life events may hurl you into a dark night of the soul, choose to be a co-pilot of your dark night adventure. Summon the courage to dislocate yourself. Choose your dislocation. I dare you to go just a little too far.

– Achim Nowak

Acknowledgements

We are so very thankful for the many colleagues, friends, and family who helped birth this book.

We are especially grateful to

- Caroline de Posada, Carl Ficks Jr., Dr. Tom Garcia, Dr. Betsy Guerra, Dr. Lynne Maureen Hurdle, Alisa Sample-Alexander, Mark J. Silverman, and Malissa Smith - for saying YES to contributing to this collection of essays, and for the exquisite honesty and power of their writing. We have been moved and inspired by their words.
- Bruce Turkel – for his thoughtful, generous and richly personal Foreword for *The Difference*.
- Donna Ratajczak - for her uncanny editorial eye, and her impeccable ability to elevate any piece of writing she touches.
- The team at Balboa Press - for their consummate professionalism in assembling this book and taking it into production.
- Hugo Sanchez Camacho – for his agility in helping us create the cover design, and for his invaluable behind-the-scenes project management during every phase of this book's creation.
- David Harleston – for his expert assistance in crafting the legal arrangements for this book.

- Alena Schabes - for appreciating the healing power of telling your story with transparency and vulnerability.
- The many authors, thinkers, and luminaries who previewed this book and showered it with praise.

– Achim Nowak and Rosemary Ravinal

Biographies

Photo by Mark Thompson

Achim Nowak (co-editor) is an executive coach, TEDx speaker, author of 3 books on personal excellence, and the host of the MY FOURTH ACT podcast. A serial entrepreneur, Achim has founded an international training and coaching firm in Florida, co-founded an acclaimed theater company in Washington DC, and trained as a mediator at the Brooklyn Courts.

Achim holds a M.A. in Organizational Psychology and International Relations from New York University and has been recognized with a PEN Syndicated Fiction Award. An earlier version of his essay in this collection was published in the Seneca Review's The Lyric Body issue.
www.achimnowak.com

Photo by Image 1st Miami

Rosemary Ravinal (co-editor) is a public speaker, executive speaker coach and TEDx presenter who works with high-profile leaders in Spanish and English. She is recognized as America's Premier Bilingual Public Speaking Coach after decades as a corporate communications leader, spokesperson and media personality in the U.S., Hispanic and Latin American markets.

In 2019, she left her role as vice president of public relations at TelevisaUnivision Network, the world's largest Spanish-language media company, to establish her consulting practice. Rosemary was born in Cuba and raised in suburban New York. In 2000, she moved to South Florida, the center of the Cuban diaspora where she is steeped in local culture and arts.

www.rosemaryravinal.com

Contributors

Carl R. Ficks, Jr., JD works with leaders to increase their effectiveness and their teams to boost engagement and productivity. The founder of No Surrender, LLC, Carl is an endurance athlete and former 30+ year trial lawyer who brings hard-won wisdom, real world experience and actionable strategies to his work.

Carl is a frequent guest on leadership, business and legal podcasts, and a sought-after corporate trainer. His "Friday Ficks" newspaper column provides strategies, tools and inspiration to stay resourceful and resilient. When not cycling crazy miles, Carl enjoys cooking and traveling with his wife and two daughters. www.carlficks.com

Dr. Tom Garcia is a soul-centered coach and transformational guide. His work is to teach, lead and guide people to awaken to their higher purpose, so that they live healthier, happier more fulfilling lives.

Tom's ability to listen deeply creates a safe, sacred space that allows you to reclaim the sacred memory of who you are. His gentle presence and clear guidance leads you past self doubt and uncertainty to clarity and peace, and draws you into the light of your own inner wisdom and authenticity. He lives in the mountains outside Durango, Colorado. www.drtomgarcia.com

Dr. Betsy Guerra is a bilingual psychotherapist, international speaker, and author of *Hurt 2 Hope: Heal the pain of loss, grief, and adversity.* She is the founder of Better with Betsy, the only platform dedicated to elevating humanity by supporting individuals through a powerful psycho-spiritual approach.

Betsy does this in her private practice, speaking career, online programs, and the Faith-Based Coaching Academy—where she trains and certifies service driven individuals as clinically competent and deeply spiritual life coaches who lead by example. Dr. Betsy has an inspiring life story, which has been featured in global media outlets such as NBC6, FOX 11, and Univision, to name a few.
www.betterwithbetsy.com

Dr. Lynne Maureen Hurdle (she/her), is a communication expert and conflict resolution strategist, diversity, equity and inclusion facilitator, writer, TEDX speaker, and leadership coach with over 40 years of experience in blending the connection between communication, conflict and culture into her unique style of engagement for leaders.

She is the author of the best seller, *Closing Conflict for Leaders: How to Be a Bold Leader and Develop a Kick-Ass, High-Functioning, Happy AF Team*. She also leads the sold-out group On The Matter of Race, a six-month journey for white people who want to learn about racism and take action.
www.lynnemaureenhurdle.com

Caroline de Posada is an international, bilingual speaker, author, and life coach who blends personal development with her gift of storytelling to inspire action in those she serves. After the death of her father, Caroline left law to carry on his legacy through coaching, speaking, and writing. Today, she focuses on wellness, mindset, and relationships, using her CORE methodology to create accountability programs.

Caroline is the founder of Caro's CORE, a community of people striving to be their best selves, and co-founder of RejuvaFAST, which incorporates scientific research on fasting and anti-aging for a whole-body approach.
www.carolinedeposada.com

Alisa Sample-Alexander is a highly qualified motivational speaker, recording artist, master facilitator, and learning professional who holds degrees from Baylor University and Texas Woman's University. Because enriching the lives of others is her passion, she considers it a privilege to have built a career and more importantly a life helping others.

She's created learning for religious settings, corporate environments, and college at Texas Woman's University. This passion for education has also provided an opportunity to co-author the textbook, *Women in Sociology*. More recently, Alisa has co-authored *My Unchanging Shepherd*, with her mother, Rubie Sample.
www.alisainspires.com

Mark J. Silverman is an Executive Coach, Speaker and the Author of the Bestselling *Only 10s 2.0 – Confront Your To- Do List, Transform Your Life* which has sold over 75,000 copies to date. He is the host of the Rising Leader Podcast and is currently working on his third book, *The Rising Leader Handbook - High Achiever ≠ Effective Leader.*

Mark leads workshops internationally, helping CEOs and Senior Leaders focus on the skills needed to lead their organizations to greater success and satisfaction.
www.markjsilverman.com

Malissa Smith is the author of *A History Of Women's Boxing*, the first comprehensive narrative of the sport The Ring magazine dubbed "The Bible of Women's Boxing."

Smith speaks and writes frequently about the sport and with her two co-hosts, developed the popular WAAR Room podcast focused on sports justice. Smith maintains positions in boxing as a founding board member of the IWBHF, an elector for the IBHOF, and as a member of the The Ring's women's ratings panel. Maintaining her own wellness, she trains at the world-renowned Gleason's Gym and writes pieces for her blog, Girlboxing.
www.girlboxing.org

Bruce Turkel has helped create some of the world's compelling brands, including Hasbro, Nike, and American Express. He is a Hall of Fame keynote speaker, author, musician, artist, and runner.

A guest expert on news outlets like CNN, he has been featured in The New York Times, Fast Company, and other publications. The latest of Bruce's six books, *Is That All There Is?* was preceded by *All About Them*, a Forbes Top-10 business book of the year. An accomplished harmonica player, he fronts the R&B band Blackstar. Bruce is an incessant doodler, famous for his caricatures of local and national business leaders. He is a dedicated — but slow — runner.
www.bruceturkel.com

Printed in the United States
by Baker & Taylor Publisher Services